D0690357

The Perfect
Job Reference

Other books by Jeffrey G. Allen, J.D., C.P.C.

HOW TO TURN AN INTERVIEW INTO A JOB
(also available on audiocassette)

FINDING THE RIGHT JOB AT MIDLIFE

THE PLACEMENT STRATEGY HANDBOOK

THE EMPLOYEE TERMINATION HANDBOOK

PLACEMENT MANAGEMENT

SURVIVING CORPORATE DOWNSIZING

THE COMPLETE Q&A JOB INTERVIEW BOOK

The Perfect Job Reference

Jeffrey G. Allen, J.D., C.P.C.

WILEY

John Wiley & Sons, Inc.

New York • Chichester • Brisbane • Toronto • Singapore

This publication is designed to provide accurate and
authoritative information in regard to the subject matter
covered. It is sold with the understanding that the
publisher is not engaged in rendering legal, accounting,
or other professional service. If legal advice or other
expert assistance is required, the services of a competent
professional person should be sought. *From a
Declaration of Principles jointly adopted by a
Committee of the American Bar Association and a
Committee of Publishers.*

Library of Congress Cataloging-in-Publication Data

Allen, Jeffrey G.
    The perfect job reference / by Jeffrey G. Allen
        p.   cm.
    Includes bibliographical references.
    ISBN 0-471-52157-4.—ISBN 0-471-52158-2 (pbk.)
    1. Employment references.   I. Title.
HF5549.5.R45A44 1990
650.14—dc20   89-70585
                                                    CIP

Printed in the United States of America

90 91 10 9 8 7 6 5 4 3 2 1

To those millions of employees haunted by ghosts of the past . . .

May this book turn those ghosts into guardian angels and genies.

Dare to dream once again.

With appreciation . . .

To my wife, Bev;
to our daughter, Angela;
to an editor's editor, Mike Hamilton,
    who conceived the book;
and to Louann Werksma,
    who assisted with its research and development.

Without you, it never would have happened.

Contents

enthusiastic, powerful fan club. We'll discuss specific ways. The results will increase your "hireability" and your confidence!

Chapter 3: Personal References: Who They Are and How to Get Them

The impact of personal references is underestimated greatly by applicants. This is because they think employers don't consider the opinions of family members and friends. They do—if the right ones are chosen. In fact, a personal reference network can actually be *more* effective than a professional one in getting someone hired. The enthusiasm and desire to help of those closest to you can be coupled with the right answers to get you hired. It just takes a little planning. This chapter shows how it's done.

Chapter 4: Perfect Professional Telephone References

If you've ever done reference checking, you know that most of the time professional references are *anything* but professional. It's not their fault—they're unprepared, uninspired, and often underwhelmed about the job you did for them. It's unfortunate and unnecessary. This chapter tells you the specific things they want and need. It's your responsibility to tell them. Now you can do it properly.

Chapter 5: Perfect Personal Telephone References

The two essentials are always credibility and knowledge about you. *Every* personal reference needs to know how to present a profile of the applicant that matches the employer's "wish list." We'll go through a step-by-step approach, then show you how to get feedback from them to ensure that their positive references will be considered. After all, who's in a better position to know you, and who wants to help you more?

Chapter 6: Elements of a Perfect Reference Letter   69

Reference letters submitted with your resume can dramatically increase the probability of being called for a job interview. They can also dramatically increase the probability of a job offer after the interviews. The reverse is also true. Once you know how to construct a reference letter properly, you can customize several for use by members of your fan club. This chapter details the elements that must be there.

Chapter 7: Examples of Perfect Reference Letters   81

The examples in this chapter give you variations of the upbeat, concise, direct pattern that every effective reference letter follows. They're balanced, believable, "better letters." Once your references start using the format, you'll start getting offer after offer. We all learned how to write by imitation. Now it's time to learn how the pros *communicate* and *motivate* in writing.

Chapter 8: Getting a Perfect Reference Letter from Your Present Supervisor   93

Whether you're about to be laid off, fired, or just want that letter for "future reference," we discuss how to get it. You have the most leverage before you leave, so let's use it to get you the best possible letter *now*. As every lawyer knows, get the witness's statement in writing—that way he or she can't change his or her story at the time of trial. Most importantly, he or she probably won't even be asked!

Chapter 9: The Perfect Solicitation Letter from a Reference   103

A little known way to use the power of third-party testimonials is the solicitation letter. It's so easy to have someone with the proper credentials write a letter about you aimed at senior executives in target companies. Recruiters call this a "broadcast letter." It's one of the most effective ways to place someone. When a properly positioned friend does it, the results are even more effective! What you write about yourself doesn't even *register* compared to the impact of what someone else writes. There's a job anywhere if the approach is right. Stand by—we're about to position you for your new position.

Even the best resumes, applications, and interviews omit items that require clarification. The inclusion letter provides this information. Whether it's a gap in employment or a report you didn't bring, this chapter shows you how to write the letter you need. Form is much more important than content on this one. It's a perfect opportunity to get yourself perfectly hired!

A follow-up letter can be much more than merely a letter-sized thank-you note. Fortunately for you, more than 95 percent of them are nothing more. If they're sent at all, they have no effect. Sometimes the wrong ones even *stop* the hiring process. So, let's go through a few alternate formats that really work. In fact, they work *so* well that they can actually turn a rejection into an acceptance. There are specific reasons for this, and we review them, too.

I got the best job of my career with one of these. Ever since, I've studied how I did it, and showed thousands of others the technique. Knowing *who* to call, *when* to call, and *how* to call can restate your image at the most crucial stage of the hiring process: the post-interview evaluation. Call the wrong person, and you might just as well be calling yourself. Call

too early or too late, and you've courteously wasted
your "one phone call." Call improperly, and you'll
hear some version of "Don't call us, we'll call you."
But call the way I suggest, and you can get the best
job of your career, too.

The law's not perfect, but it is extremely powerful.
For you, knowledge is power. We cover how to use
the explosive wrongful termination, defamation,
invasion of privacy, and conspiracy laws to get you
reference letters as good as your own right away—
in fact, *write* away! Your secret's safe with me.

You'd be amazed at how much information on your
personal, financial, and occupational activities is in
the files and computer memories of local, state, and
federal agencies. Much of it is there for the asking,
and employers ask constantly. Shouldn't you know
what they know? Here's how to find out—and
remove or correct those "imperfections."

It's perfectly logical to try to conceal a criminal
arrest or conviction. Nobody's perfect. Employers
know this, so they check public records. You know
it, so you interview poorly. Then you're mysteriously rejected or gently "ejected" without knowing
why. With a little help, you can probably have those
records officially sealed forever.

About the Author

Jeffrey G. Allen, J.D., C.P.C., is America's leading placement attorney. Direct experience as a certified placement counselor, personnel manager, and professional negotiator uniquely qualifies him to write the first book ever on obtaining the best job reference possible.

Mr. Allen is Director of the National Placement Law Center in Los Angeles and author of more bestselling books in the career field than anyone else. Among them are *How to Turn an Interview into a Job, Finding the Right Job at Midlife, The Placement Strategy Handbook, Placement Management,* and *The Complete Q&A Job Interview Book.* He writes a nationally syndicated column entitled "Placements and the Law," conducts seminars, and is regularly featured in television, radio, and newspaper interviews.

Mr. Allen has been appointed Special Advisor to the American Employment Association, is General Counsel to the California Association of Personnel Consultants, and is nationally recognized as the foremost authority in the specialty of placement law.

Introduction

The most elusive phase of the placement process is also the most devastating—the reference check.

The powerful third-party role of a reference can be either terrific or terrible, depending on you. Your reference check doesn't have to be a *test* (that you take blindly, wondering if you'll "pass"); it can be a *testimonial*. A properly constructed reference letter can get you an interview, and a properly *instructed* reference can get you hired.

But are your references prepared? Do you even know who they will be? Are *you* prepared? Do you realize that a reference letter is a fully controllable, direct-mail marketing device that has statistically verifiable results? Have you ever studied the proven, potent techniques that move people to buy every product or service imaginable? Aren't *you* a product being sold in the labor market? Aren't your *services* being sold, too?

During the past decade, obtaining perfect references has required more sophistication. As I noted in *How to Turn an Interview into a Job*:

> "Reference checking" is really descriptive of what goes on. During the past decade, statutory and case law in the areas of equal employment, unemployment insurance, consumer disclosure, credit reporting, libel, slander, privacy, interference with contractual relations, and wrongful termination has increased geometrically.
>
> This has led most corporate attorneys to advise against furnishing any references on behalf of former employees. The result is that the majority of applicants

have no professional references. Those that do are left with cautious, impersonal, passive reporters. Your ability to develop a cadre of interested, articulate, active advocates will be like opening your engine full throttle.[1]

Employers want to hire the best people—they don't care about the reference's liability. So, they continue asking and they continue receiving strange responses. Human nature is a reality that doesn't yield to regulation. If it did, the National Placement Law Center would have drafted a law long ago that prohibited any reference checking at all.

The crime would be a form of gambling—"reference roulette"—held in a career casino with the highest stakes imaginable. Livelihoods would be on the line with every spin.

Juries would be instructed to consider convictions when:

1. The person calling does not know what to ask.

2. The person calling does not listen carefully to the responses.

3. The person calling does not fully understand the response.

4. The person calling is looking for a reason not to hire the applicant.

5. The reference does not know the applicant well enough to respond validly.

6. The reference does not know the applicant at all.

7. The reference is thinking of someone else who is less qualified than the applicant.

8. The reference understates the applicant's qualifications so that he or she can apply for the job himself or herself.

9. The reference has a hidden agenda to interfere with the applicant's future employment.

10. The reference *says* one thing and *conveys* another.

My first job after graduating from college was working with someone who charged a fee for independently checking references. I'd review his notes and prepare formal reports for his clients. While I couldn't tell you much about the references beyond their names and phone numbers, I could tell you a lot about how my boss felt that day. Like every reference checker and every reference before and after, he held the applicant's job—his or her livelihood—in his humanly frail hands.

Reference checking *itself* is not a crime. Only the most obvious improper questions and responses invoke liability. Then it's often too late to save someone's career. Job applicants don't know they've been walking around under a rain cloud until they're drowning.

Now, once and for all, you can do something about it. In the pages that follow, you'll see how easily references can be turned into testimonials. That's right—you can actually rig that random, revolving roulette wheel. It's perfectly legal and perfectly professional. In fact, it should be the *employee's* affirmative action law!

So, without delay, let's even the odds toward our objective of perfect references. "Luck" has nothing to do with it. As the roulette dealer says when the wheel's about to stop, "No more bets."

Best wishes for career success!

Chapter

1

Ten Times When Employers *Will* Check References

You'll probably be surprised, but not as surprised as you'll be to typical answers to this true-false exam:

1. Nobody checks references anymore.

2. Nobody really cares about references.

3. I've always been friendly with my coworkers and bosses, so I don't have to worry about what they'll say.

It might as well be a multiple-choice exam. The answer would be, "None of the above."

If you think any of these statements is true, you're probably *still* looking for the right job. You're not the only one. It is safe to say a good *50 percent* of jobseekers are doomed to failure—or at best to boredom—simply because they aren't aware of the importance of the *right* references at the *right* time.

It's *not* true that interviewers are too busy to check references. It's *not* true that people don't believe the references they're given. It's *not* true that you can expect even the friendliest friends to clearly, concisely, credibly, and consistently deliver their potent "third-party testimonial."

References—both personal and professional—are a vital element in your self-marketing plan. In fact, they're *more* important than ever.

WHY THE EMPLOYER CHECKS REFERENCES

There are several reasons.

First, hiring today is a costly proposition. Turnover affects the bottom line. Getting the right person for the right job every time is a righteous corporate objective.

Second, the workplace has changed. When the nation's economy was based on manufacturing, people were members of trades and craft guilds. There were objective standards: the journeyman's card, the master mechanic's license, and the customary apprenticeship requirement.

Today we *think* for a living. We are in the age of the "knowledge worker." Too often, the right buzzwords can mask a lack of knowledge in the limited time available for interviewing. With thousands of new areas of specialization, the interviewer in the personnel office can't be certain an applicant knows what he or she is talking about.

Therefore, your past performance, technical understanding, and skill level must be verified, independent of your resume and interviewing ability, *before* you get recommended for a second, more serious, interview.

The third element that has increased the importance of references is today's mobile society. We no longer grow up, marry, work, and retire in the same towns where we were born and where our ancestors were born. In fact, most people are better known in their *industries* than in their neighborhoods. "He comes from a good family," and "I've known her all my life," are hardly ever said or written by references anymore.

That can work to your benefit. Instead of being held hostage by a lifelong (or perhaps generation-long) reputation that merely reflects random impressions of you, with careful selection and development of references, you can market the image *you* want hirers to see.

In our post-industrial age, "referencing"—a potent form of advertising—is your competitive edge. In fact, referencing is probably the only way an employer can read between the lines of your resume, probe beyond your interview performance, and ascertain whether you're "real." Of course, all they know is what you'll show.

References are among the most misunderstood, mis-handled, and missed areas of the hiring process. Without com-plete knowledge of—and control over—*who* says *what* about you *when* and *how*, you may be walking around under a storm cloud and never know that it's about to reference rain.

What your references *say* isn't as important as what they *convey*. Even an apparently benign statement such as, "His work performance was satisfactory," can be interpreted in a way that will stop a job offer cold.

How about the response to, "Can you tell me anything about her work habits and attitude?" A simple "No" is all it takes to generate "No Interest Letter No. 2." The reason may be as simple as a policy, drafted by the company's defensive legal department, permitting only disclosure of employment. If you don't know that and compensate for it, you'll be sorry you opened the mail.

Tragedies like this are unnecessary, especially since favorable, credible personal and professional references can be readily identified, nurtured, and trained to whisk you from the street into the seat.

TEN SITUATIONS WHEN REFERENCES WILL BE CHECKED

Although you must conduct your job search assuming that references will *always* be checked, here are ten situations where you can be almost certain it will happen. Half concern the type of employer. The other half relate to the type of applicant. Look for your own situation in them.

Employers

1. Companies with Overstaffed Personnel Departments

As a rule, if there is more than one full-time personnel type for every 250 employees in the company, the employer is overstaffed (and overstuffed) in that department. Personnelers, therefore, have the time to track down the references, get them to talk (an increasingly time-consuming activity), go through a comprehensive review of the candidate's attributes, and transcribe their notes.

They also have time to justify their existence. As a result, they'll be tempted to write long, narrative, "interpretive" work-ups similar to those used by psychoanalysts. Since their agenda has more to do with their job than yours, reference reality yields to recruiting rhetoric.

In conducting your research on companies you're considering, check the "employee-employment" ratio. When you find a company with 10,000 employees and an employment staff of 100 (a 100:1 ratio) alert your references. They can dramatically influence that recruiting rhetoric by a rehearsed recommendation. Really! I'll show you how in the pages that follow.

2. Financial Institutions

I was recruited from a personnel manager's job by a major bank to become a legal assistant without anyone even checking my *pulse*! That was around 15 years ago, and an exception even then. It still happens—but it won't happen just by wishing for it.

Today, the financial industry is regulated more than any other. Checking references is SOP. *Not* checking them is heresy. This category includes commercial banks, savings and loans, finance companies, stockbrokers, accounting firms, credit-reporting agencies, and other fiduciaries that handle money or financial data for others. Your references should emphasize trustworthiness, ethics, conservatism, discretion, and balanced judgment.

3. High-Tech Companies

Even small high-tech companies with no personnel staff tend to check references thoroughly. Protective of their proprietary innovations, high-tech companies of all sizes are the major customers for outside private investigation services. Of course, nobody talks about it; but it gets the job done fast, and all the investigator needs is a car. This is business as usual in the cloak-and-dagger world of high-tech businesses.

It's not unusual for investigators hired by such companies to visit an applicant's neighbors and, using an assumed identity and any number of "routines," find out everything from the way you walk to the type of trash you have.

If a disgruntled neighbor was unhappy about the noise at your last backyard bash or *thinks* you have strange friends (everybody's strange to someone else), you'll be slippin' and slidin' on the sidewalks of Silicon Street. So, if Silicon Valley is where you'd like to live, do your homework before you arrive.

4. Government Contractors

Government contractors are compulsively careful about detailed background investigations. When it comes to "personnel procurement," the thicker the files, the happier the auditor.

In most cases, you will complete a *Personnel Security Questionnaire* (PSQ), which will be verified in a thorough check of educational institutions, armed services, employers, and acquaintances. If a security clearance is required for your job, you will be finger-printed and checked even further through FBI and other records.

It's imperative to make a *full disclosure* of everything, since government contractors won't hire and will fire for any "material misrepresentation." That includes any omission of derogatory public records. We'll discuss how to handle this more fully in Chapters 14 and 15.

5. High-Turnover Companies

In the old days, "hire-'em-fire-'em" companies didn't care. It was SRO in the employment lobby. But now you can hear a handshake. The "cost-per-hire" amount regularly averages five figures. And that excludes relocation, hire-on bonuses, and other inducements.

So, if you're applying to a company that has a history of high turnover (whether from misguided management, immoral morale, or any other factor), it must close the revolving door. Reference checking is a logical way.

These employers carefully check candidates who have a history of jobhopping. If that's you, be sure your references can factually explain legitimate reasons why you made so many career moves.

That ends our review of the five types of *companies* that are likely to reference check. Now, for the five types of *candidates* almost *any* employer will check.

Candidates

6. Applicants Who Rattle Their References' Skeletons During the Interview

Self-incrimination is the most common way an employer discovers a regrettable reference. In fact, it's the most common way *any* investigator gets information—directly from the "subject."

In *Interviewing for the Decision Maker*, Lawrence O'Leary explained why:

[T]here is a certain amount of logic to the idea that the person who is most familiar with the candidate's performance is the candidate himself . . .

[T]he richness of the interview is in a great part due to the interviewer's option to follow up on responses which may suggest additional questions and further probing.[1]

An interviewer can spot just what O'Leary is talking about when he or she asks a question like, "Who was your immediate supervisor?" or "Do you mind if we contact a few of your former coworkers?" A loud clanking sound usually occurs. The applicant writhes in pain.

Clean your closet *before* you're asked. If there are skeletons in there, dust them off, dress them up, and give them some dancing lessons.

7. Applicants Who Don't Favorably Impress the Interviewer

This category includes the candidate who looks too young to have the lengthy, in-depth experience on his resume; the one with unexplained gaps in her employment record; the single parent who has not arranged for responsible, reliable child care; the distracted applicant who reveals he is going through a divorce and then gives personal details the interviewer doesn't want (and shouldn't have).

If you don't interview well, your references may rehabilitate you. Just work harder to prepare them, since the interviewer's attitude will be one of "prove me right" rather than "prove me wrong."

Overworked, underpaid interviewers welcome the opportunity to screen out a marginal candidate. With a negative opinion from a bombed interview, they just need a reason to go on to the next applicant—they want that requisition off their desk and out of their lives. Someone who can't self-market won't be able to go the distance in subsequent interviews. References are a *supportive* marketing technique—verification of your sales pitch, not sales tools in themselves.

If you don't feel confident about your interviewing technique, pick up a copy of my paperbacks *How To Turn an Interview into a Job* and *The Complete Q&A Job Interview Book*. Commit them to memory, and you'll never explode, fizzle, or otherwise bomb in an interview again.

8. Applicants Who Have Not Been Pre-Sold

If you're working with an executive recruiter, you're probably (but only partially) pre-sold. Working with headhunters can provide some advantages to a job candidate. They can play a major role in your success. Headhunters know the true decision makers in a company and understand what they want in an employee. The headhunter can give you an introduction and help you prove your qualifications for the position.

If you are not working with a headhunter, pre-sell yourself in your initial phone and mail contacts. Do this well, and you'll enhance the effect of favorable references.

9. Candidates Who Have Not Held Similar Jobs

Since hundreds of new types of jobs are created daily, more and more people apply for jobs they haven't held before. Further, structural unemployment moves many to find jobs in other industries.

What interviewer wouldn't check references on a teacher or social worker who is applying for a sales position? Even design engineers who apply for technical supervisory jobs are suspect. There is just not enough "comparability" to convey "jobseeker credibility."

Because they are usually interviewed more intensively (even if the company has actively recruited them), and because they frequently get to the interview stage with less understanding of the job, such applicants also tend to rattle the reference skeletons mentioned in item 6.

Determine which basic skills and abilities from your current (former) profession will cross over to the targeted job. Study the company. If possible, talk to people in similar jobs and familiarize yourself with what they do. It's probably a lot like what you've done. Over 90 percent of all jobs are common sense. The remaining 10 percent usually require a certification or license, so you probably won't be applying for those anyway.

Haven't you ever looked at some successful person and thought, "I can do that!" Now you know why: There's a 90 percent chance you were right.

If you're changing fields, a good book to read is *When Apples Aren't Enough* by Jean Miller and Georgianna Dickinson, two refugees from the professions of teaching, counseling, and library science.

10. Applicants with Unusual Job-Changing Patterns

A candidate whose job history reveals either less or more than the *average* tenure for *similar* jobs with a prospective employer will trip a reference check. If the company you're applying with has an average employee tenure of five years, and you have either significantly less or significantly more years in your former or present jobs, be prepared. The greater the variance from the average, the higher the probability that reference checking will occur.

The once-every-other-year jobhopper is a natural for an inquiry. But someone who's stayed in the same job at the same company for ten years will look strange, too.

Arm yourself with information about average tenure with the target employer. Then, volunteer a convincing explanation about why your background moved around more or less *before* the references are asked. (Obviously, make sure your references understand and agree with your explanation, too.)

These are the ten typical situations where your references will be checked. Fortunately (from now on), they're not the only ones.

START NETWORKING NOW

Before you schedule interviews, review your job history in detail. If necessary, inspect and rebuild any bridges you burned.

A few phone calls will help you assess your RQ (reference quotient). If the former supervisor you'll rely on for a job answers your phone greeting with "Elaine who?", you have some reacquainting to do.

The best time to start building a system of references is from the day you get your first job. Although most of us neglect this important area, it's never too late to reconnect with our past.

The following chapters comprise a step-by-step instruction manual for establishing, maintaining, and maximizing a reference network. We begin in Chapter 2 with "Professional References: Who They Are and How to Get Them."

Chapter

2

Professional References: Who They Are and How to Get Them

Most jobseekers neglect 80 percent of their potential references, silencing a crowd of eyewitnesses who could have testified on their behalf to persuade the job judge. When the time comes to ask for references, they consider only two sources—former supervisors and instructors. These people may know you well, and they may be the references most employers check with first. But they aren't your *only* references—and they might not qualify for your fan club without being initiated. In fact, they comprise only about 20 percent of your potential "witness list."

It is much easier to assemble references from that 80 percent. Few people begin a job search *after* giving notice to their present employer. In most organizations, once you've announced your intentions to leave, you're no longer considered part of the team. In fact, you're lucky if they let you stay until your termination date! Former friends and suspicious supervisors watch you as though you're a shoplifter.

You must carefully review your past to list other sources. As you do this, you relive your accomplishments. This boosts your confidence and reminds you how great you are. Before long, you'll be looking forward to renewing old acquaintances.

TAKE INVENTORY

Begin your witness list by taking a careful look back at your career. (You should do this anyway when updating your resume.) Roll your rolodex and dig in your drawers for those brochures, business cards, or notes from people you met on assignments, at seminars, or at conventions—people you meant to contact but never did. Find them and list their names and phone numbers.

Then review the papers and files in your desk drawers for names of influential people—at your company and others— who saw you in action and were impressed with what they saw. Contractors, suppliers, and colleagues in other divisions of the company—even highly placed professionals with your company's customers—all are potential reference gold.

Once you start digging, you'll realize that there's no bottom to the mine. In *How to Turn an Interview into a Job*, I advised that:

> Work-related references are generally more potent than academic ones, because business wants tangible services. A bright, positive coworker can also be used effectively and will tend to identify with your needs. As with personal references, you should obtain their consent and review their "testimony." Don't let them use the old, "Don't worry, I'll just tell them a bunch of lies" routine to get you off the phone. This is a *business* matter, and you will reciprocate.[1]

Your list of potential professional references includes, but is not limited to, the following:

- Your present supervisor (if your job search is known).
- Your former supervisors.
- Your boss's boss and other high-level executives at present or past employers who have seen your work or presentations.
- Coworkers at present or past employers who know your skills and effectiveness.

- Subordinates who can testify to your management ability.

- Coworkers or others who have served with you on committees or task forces.

- Members of trade associations or other professional groups who know you.

- Managers of support departments who have worked with you to service your department. These include managers of departments such as Human Resources, Finance, Management Information Systems, Communications, Sales, Marketing, Market Research, Purchasing, Inventory Control, and so on.

CALLING IN YOUR MARKERS

If you have been vigilant about cultivating a network of professional contacts—kept in touch with people you met on the road, sent congratulations when colleagues received promotions or awards, and notified them about projects that interested them—you have it made. All you have to do now is start smiling and dialing.

The Initial Telephone Call

Your telephone script should be something like this:

Joe, good to hear your voice again! It's Sam Stone. Did you get that article I sent last month on semiconductor research?

(Friendly greeting, grateful acknowledgment)

My pleasure. I wasn't sure if you subscribed to that journal, and I thought the article might relate to your area.

But, I have another reason for calling. I'll only keep you a minute. I've decided it's time to move on. The reorganization here has limited the opportunity for advancement, so I've decided to look around for a director position. This is confidential, of course.

Since we've worked closely together in the past, I'd be honored if you'd provide a professional reference. Your great reputation in the industry would help to verify *my* credentials. Will you assist me?

(Typical reply:)

Sure, Sam! I'd be delighted. I'm sorry to hear you're not moving into that director position you were counting on at Company X. But, someone like you is bound to land on his feet in no time—probably in an even better slot. Not only will I provide a reference, I'll keep my eyes and ears open for you. Now, what do you need. A letter? Or do you just want me to be on the ready for phone calls?

I'm not sure yet. But I'll send my resume today, along with a brief summary of the work we did together on ———— project, just to refresh you. There's also a list of questions you'll probably be asked. I'll get those out to you today, and I'll call you to discuss both the letter and telephone reference about the middle of next week? Sound okay?

Sure, great! Only I'll be out of town the following week. When do you expect these calls to start coming?

I'm not sure. I haven't lined up any interviews yet, but I expect to start late next week. I'll drop you a note when I do, with names of companies I'm considering.

Sounds great, Sam—and good luck. I'm looking forward to getting that resume. In fact, send me a few copies. Our senior vice president is retiring at the end of the year, and I think they are going to search outside for the openings that will result. Word around here is the jobs aren't going to be filled from within. I know of a few managers who'd like to see your resume.

Thanks! Please keep me posted. I wouldn't mind moving over to your area at all. Are you still a tennis superstar?

No, no . . . time and work have taken their toll on my tennis game. It might be nice to have an old competitor around to keep me in shape, though.

I'm really looking forward to that possibility, Joe. I'll address the envelope now. It should be on your desk in two days.

Great, Sam. Talk to you soon.

Not only did you obtain a credible reference, but you now have a well-connected talent scout who will assist in your job search. This is a natural outcome of asking someone for assistance. Remember that almost *every* person you call works for someone else. *Everyone* might be looking for a job tomorrow. There's a powerful identification with jobseekers, and a mutual need for references. It brings out the best in human nature—helping someone else.

Standard job-hunting calls like, "Hi, Joe. I'm looking to make a job change," usually encounter silence followed by a reply that sounds like this:

Gee, Sam, I'd like to help you, but I just don't know of anything right now. Why don't you send me a resume, and I'll keep you in mind for future openings.

The result? The shaft rather than the gold.

But when you call to ask for a reference, you're asking for something your colleague can give readily, at no cost and little inconvenience. He or she is flattered and it feels great to help. That's why he or she will try to generate leads for interviews, too. The more influential the contact, the more likely this will happen.

The Let-Me-Refresh-Your-Memory Lunch

The conversation should end differently if you're near the contact. Then, when asked, "What should I say?" you reply:

> **I have a resume and a few notes I've prepared to make it easy. I'd like to take you out for lunch next week and go over the details with you. How about if I pick you up next Tuesday at 11:30?**

Either Tuesday or another day, the lunch date will be arranged; and, for a minimum "retainer," you have a personal *personnel* consultant who'll actively help you with jobseeking. Even if he or she does nothing more than provide a rehearsed reference, it will be the best investment you can ever make— an investment in *yourself*.

In Chapter 4 we discuss how to prepare your colleague to give you the perfect telephone reference. Chapter 6 reviews the elements of the perfect reference *letter*. Do your homework and prepare your notes about the things your colleague knows about your work. Don't ask anyone to give information about you that they don't know—but tell them *everything* you want them to know!

It's all done with mirrors and lights—completed application forms and resumes. Employers only know what you show.

When Contacts Have Been Neglected

Did you burn a few bridges? Do you even *know*? You'd better; some prospective employer will try to cross one of them for sure. Retrace your steps by phone and track down those negative or "unpositive" references before you continue along your career path.

Almost *everybody* has burned bridges. But almost *nobody* repairs them. That's great news for you. Those bridge-burners don't have a clue about why they're being rejected time after time. Their resumes get favorable responses, they interview well, and they're sure an offer's on its way. Then they receive a rejection letter in the mail or—even worse—nothing.

If that's a familiar experience, learn from it. Repair those bridges now, reinforce them, and make periodic maintenance checks. Promise yourself that from now on you're going to keep your fan club active and growing.

In *How to Turn an Interview into a Job*, I urged:

> Professional references should be called, courted, and remembered during the holiday season. They shared an important part of your life and can be a great source of guidance and perspective. Although the years and distance have separated us, I am still only a telephone call away from my first supervisor, and all that followed; two became dear friends . . . life is too short.[2]

Call or send notes once or twice a year. Keep current on professional news and notes. Congratulate when you hear about a promotion or award. Commiserate when something unfortunate happens. Share the wealth when you get free theater or game tickets.

PREPARING YOUR "SALES FORCE"

Now let's get your references ready to sell you and your attributes. *Scour* your memory. Sit down with old calendars, files, letters—*anything* that will trigger the names of people who will be good reference prospects. Don't think only of jobs, but of specific tasks within each job.

Relax in a comfortable chair. Close your eyes. Think about your accomplishments, achievements, and awards. As you're reliving those memories, mentally search for the faces of those who were there. Who would impress a prospective employer? The more the better—employers are easily impressed. So few "references" really are impressive.

Next, take a sheet of blank paper and write these headings across the top:

My Employer & Title	Project/ Accomplishment	Name of Reference	Current Title & Employer	Phone No.
Sample:				
Acme Mfg., Sales Director	Developed & produced new product catalog	Donna Smith	Account Exec. White Advtg.	(913) 234-5678

In this example, the reference is a key employee of your current employer's advertising agency. She worked with you on creative development, budgeting, scheduling, and producing your company's first color product catalog. She can attest (as in "testify"—under oath) to your grasp of creative concepts, ability to manage a project from beginning to end, bring it in under budget, and finish it on time. She knows that, as a result of the initial mailing of the catalog, sales increased by 50 percent.

Here there's an added incentive. Since you were instrumental in helping the company win the contract (resulting in her commission), she owes you a favor. It's not unusual, since most successes in business affect others.

This is just one example of dozens of people in your workwebs whom you must now bring forward into your consciousness.

Let's start with Donna. You haven't talked to her in about three months, since she was reassigned to other accounts. The sample script that follows will help you renew your acquaintance and get a reliable reference in the same, brief telephone conversation:

(You dial. Telephone rings. Someone picks up the line and says:)

This is Donna Smith.

Hello, Donna! This is Fred Johnson, from Acme. How have you been?

Hi, Fred. I've been good, thanks. It's been hectic since I took over our national accounts department.

(She has an even better title now; that'll look good for you!)

Congratulations. I'd heard you were moving up! Nobody deserves it more.

Thanks. And how is everything at Acme? Is the new marketing plan working for you?

It's working really well. Sales are up, and we have another mailing going out soon. The new account executive from White is working very hard. Of course, nobody will ever quite fill your shoes.

I really miss everyone at Acme. It was always a pleasure making a call there.

Donna, it's because of our great working relationship on that catalog project that I'm calling you. I've decided to make a career move. I'd like to get into a bigger operation, with national marketing and market research departments.

Well, congratulations, Fred. (Her voice is guarded; she

thinks you want a lead for a job at her company or a client.)
How can I help?

**I haven't said anything to anyone else yet. I'm trusting you
to keep this *very* confidential. I thought I'd test the water
first. I'd like to use your name as a reference, if I might.**

Well, sure, Fred! (Whew! A *reference*. No sweat!) Have
anyone call. I'll be glad to tell them you're a real pro. I
never saw anyone take a concept and turn it into a quality
product in less time.

It was so hard to believe you'd never produced a catalog
before. You were supervising our location shoots like
you'd done it all your life! I was *really* impressed with how
quickly you learned, and what a knack you had for the
creative process . . . as well as keeping an eye on the
bottom line! What do you want me to say when they call?

**Well, basically, you just said it! But, I typed up a summary
of that project, completed an application form from the
stationery store, updated my resume, and prepared a list of
questions you'll probably be asked. I can drop them off at
your office on my way to work tomorrow. Will you be in
at 8:30? I'd like to go over them with you. It'll only take
a few minutes.**

Make it 8:00 at the coffee shop downstairs and we'll have
breakfast. My treat! It will be a good-luck send off for your
job search. Okay?

You're on. Thanks—see you tomorrow morning.

That wasn't so hard, was it? Hold on though. You're not
done! Repeat that last step at least 11 more times.

A Numbers Game

Reference roulette is for rookies. Realists remember, rout and
ring at least a dozen people. They know that they're never sure

who will be called, and whether they'll call back. They heed the words of William Lareau in *Conduct Expected: The Unwritten Rules for a Successful Business Career*:

> Even if the people where you work[ed] are reasonably decent and intelligent, they can't be trusted. People aren't their best at work. Most of them are there not because they love it but because they have no choice. Yet almost all of us are forced by recurring hunger pangs and a reluctance to sleep in the rain to drag ourselves to some boring, mundane job day after day and year after year. The consequence is that people come to work with a lot of frustration, anger, and disappointment. Like caged tigers, they are limited to pacing back and forth, forced to try to control their energy and emotions as they perceive that the world is going by without them. . . . The jungle floor is carpeted with the bones of careers whose owners let down their guards.[3]

Lock up at least *six* references suitable for framing—those who are glad to hear from you, and whose wondrous words will improve your chances of getting that target job. If you don't have at least a half-dozen, half-crazed, wide-eyed professional references to take with you into an interview, call *more*!

Cross off people who greet you with, "Joe Who?" and who never seem to understand that you're not from the unemployment office. Cut the call short when the prospective reference speaks unintelligibly or calls you something unkind. Search until you find the motivated maniacs who will be glad to help you. Be sure there are no hidden agendas (such as reference revenge on jolly jobseekers).

Your references must mention the attributes and skills that will get you hired. The owner of the garage where you worked during college might be able to comment on your ability to adjust a carburetor. But, if you're supposed to be an expert in process control, that reference needs a tune-up! Help him to remember your promptness, mechanical genius, and ability to complete your work properly. If you don't put the rabbits in his hat, don't expect him to pull them out. All the words in the world won't replace the few magic ones you tell him.

Just by living, every person develops a cadre of references—known and unknown, good and bad. We're just ensuring they'll be *known*, then *good*. Let's say one job requires an ability to supervise. You trot out all the references who can attest to your management skills. Another job might require analytical skills. Revive the staff accountant from your last job. Resuscitate a statistics professor who taught a graduate course you took. Think ahead, so your reference roll reflects everyone who will be important when the roll is called.

Words to the Wise

There's an inviolate rule of business that applies to references:

"Nothing happens until somebody sells something."

We've talked about *everybody*, but now it's time to find the *somebodies* to sell you well. You must select your references with care—not so much for what they *say*, but *how* they say it.

A person who knows nothing about you can sell you as well as someone who does. This shouldn't surprise you—just turn on your TV. Does the announcer really use the laundry detergent? Does the celebrity really drive the station wagon? Does the cat really dance when he sees the dry food? No—there's another motivator. A *big* one. It motivates them to motivate you. If the words, "This is a dramatization" were required, almost every commercial would have them.

I'm not advising you to fabricate references—or for your references to fabricate facts—but this illustrates how easily the game can be rigged. Your phone calls and meetings with your prospects will help you identify the most positive, articulate, convincing ones.

Former Supervisors

Prospective employers will want to hear from your former supervisors. They will think better of you if your list of references contains their names. As I wrote in *How to Turn an Interview into a Job*:

> If you are like most applicants, you've burned a few bridges along the way. Passive-aggressive references can be even more destructive than those that make negative comments. The reason is that the interviewer does not have the opportunity to consider the source. Former supervisors are often called without your permission or even knowledge, and you may be walking around under a cloud and not know it.
>
> You know if you and your former supervisor didn't exactly need to be chiseled apart. That negative excess baggage is carried around in your unconscious. . . . Don't let it stay in your memory center . . . call and make your peace as soon as possible with every former supervisor you can find. Let them know you *really* need them![4]

REFERENCE REPAIR

If you were fired, resigned under duress, or left in the heat of battle, it's time to roll out your reference regalia. It needs repair.

Even if you don't voluntarily disclose your former supervisor's name, don't think he or she won't be called. Many companies check all past employers. If you know (or suspect) that someone is just waiting for a chance to dump a little reference rubble on your records, you have two alternatives:

1. Have someone call pretending to be an employer seeking a reference. Determine exactly what is being said about you. If it's not the best sales job possible, call

back two days later and use the technique we discussed earlier. Most lukewarm references are the result of unidentified, untrained, unmotivated folks who just need a call from you. If you don't give them a reason to help or guidance about how to do it, don't expect them to extend themselves.

2. Confront your accuser. Telephone him or her, and be firm and forthright. Make sure your conversation is liberally sprinkled with the following legalese: *interference with contractual relations, interference with prospective economic advantage, defamation of character, slander, libel, fraud, conspiracy, punitive damages, exemplary damages, attorney's fees, costs of suit, litigation,* and *jury trial.* Nice talk. It not only makes you feel great, but it works even greater.

It is not likely that you'll receive an apology, though. Instead, you'll receive denials and promises to sell well. Tell the reference that you'll be checking up on him. It'll drive him crazy waiting for a call so he can sell his little heart out. Coach him, too. Tell him what to say—he's gonna love it.

Find someone else in the same company who will give a good reference, too. Confronted references sometimes appear to be *contrived* ones. They have a tendency to crawl through the phone. Savvy personnelers "dual check" when they're suspicious.

WHEN YOUR PRESENT EMPLOYER KNOWS YOU ARE LEAVING

If you have embarked on a job search with your current employer's blessings (or in answer to its prayers), negotiate a favorable reference *before you leave.* This is particularly effective if the employer wants you to leave. Since you're cooperating, the company should be willing to give you a carefully worded reference in your favor. Ask—they rarely refuse. Then type a letter (on company letterhead) that emphasizes the positive aspects of your tenure, and prepare it for the signature of the highest ranking, most upbeat, genuinely interested person you can find. People dread writing reference letters but sign them willingly. Chapter 8 tells you exactly how to do this.

Then tell the reference (and other possibles) that they may be called. Drop a completed application, a resume, and a script on them.

In Chapters 4, 5, and 6, I detail exactly what your references (oral and written) should do. But now it's on to Chapter 3, where I turn everything you've ever heard about personal references upside down.

Chapter

3

Personal References: Who They Are and How to Get Them

In *How to Turn an Interview into a Job*, I rewrote the definition of personal references as "those dependent on you for support or who owe you money." That is not *my* definition of a personal reference, but rather the prevailing attitude of most interviewers and other human resourcers. For years, the names on an application form under "Personal References" were people no self-respecting employer would consider. Even today, over 40 percent of the time, one of the names also appears under "Person to Contact in Case of Emergency."

How to Turn an Interview into a Job also noted the potency of personal references: "[In view of the] constraints upon professional references by standard operating procedures, policies, and their own fears, . . . you should not foreclose this option."[1]

That was five years ago. Since then, personal references have become *preference references*—the winner's edge in the placement race. This chapter shows you how to use them most effectively. You'll obtain letters from "influential," "successful" people who associate with you because they *want* to, not because it's required in their work.

The interviewer will call the reference's business and receive an enthusiastic, in-depth, candid response that can't be equaled by professional references. It's like the difference between listening to a CD and a scratchy old 78. Those references come alive—they *penetrate* into the mind of the listener. And they motivate him or her to hire.

SELECTION IS KEY

The most important thing to remember is the *quality* of the reference. Don't be afraid to give your spouse's name, if he or she fits the criteria given here.

Each of your personal references should:

1. Formally consent to give a reference on your behalf.

2. Have a surname different from yours (whether related or not).

3. Work in an office where he or she can receive calls during regular business hours and, without distraction, discuss you knowledgeably, intelligently, and enthusiastically.

4. Be thoroughly prepared by you to give a knowledgeable, favorable, inspirational response.

YOUR PERSONAL FORTUNE 50

Take out a sheet of paper and list 50 friends, acquaintances, neighbors, and others you see socially or otherwise outside work. Yes, *fifty*. Remember, this is a numbers game. From that 50 you're going to screen and sort to arrive at the top *five*.

Include everyone from your current "best friend" to casual acquaintances. Try not to go back more than five years, because employers accept current references' representations more readily. Then add business advisers such as your attorney, accountant, banker, and so forth. How about community leaders? Are there people you know in your service club or gym? Do you get along with the principals and teachers at the schools your children attend? Do you at least know their *names*? Good! They qualify.

Now, scope out each one in your mind. You're looking for three characteristics:

1. A successful professional life.

2. A self-confident, outgoing demeanor.

3. Good oral and written communications skills.

Oh . . . and a fourth characteristic: They like you (or can, with a little PR).

While personal references can be located anywhere, it's helpful if they're known and respected in the community where you are conducting your job search. This allows you to leverage their favorable reputations, since they "precede them." Often, the person doing the reference checking wants to speak with prominent people in the area, so the reference will more readily be called.

If you've kept your personal life personal, you'll find this part of the process more difficult. But it's actually *easier* to obtain references who don't know you well! Ironically, strangers who are approached are more receptive. They have no negative impressions and are flattered that they are well regarded.

Someone who takes the time to talk with the banker after closing a loan; who has invited the school principal out for coffee after a PTA meeting or who volunteers for civic activities and cultivates the acquaintances made will probably have a list far longer than 50. It's so easy to find names! Just look at your local newspaper or Chamber of Commerce directory.

In picking the top 5 from the 50, choose those likely to be receptive to your request, accessible, and properly positioned to turn calls into job offers.

MAKING THE CALLS

There is no need to feel awkward about asking a total stranger for a personal reference. What's a "stranger" anyway? Just a friend you haven't met. We're all just passin' through on our way to that great job-hunting ground in the sky. Like professional references, your personal references will be complimented that, from among all the people you know, you selected them to recommend you. If some of them aren't, don't use them. Considering that the list is infinite, these people are expendable.

Try a script similar to the following conversation between Betty, a jobseeker, and Howard, an attorney who lives in her neighborhood and who campaigned with her last year for a budget increase to improve schools in their city:

Howard, this is Betty Brown.

Hi, Betty! I've been meaning to call and ask you what you're using on your roses this year. They look great.

Why, thank you! I'll have to refer that question to the family gardener. Frank takes care of the yard.

I'd really like to know. I haven't had any luck with mine. What can I do for you?

Well, I just passed the CPA exam, and I want to make a career move now. Foster Plastics is a great company, and it was convenient to work in town while the kids were young. But now I'm ready for a larger organization. I thought I'd target the insurance industry.

Sounds, good. Congratulations on your certification. That was a lot of work. I wish I knew someone to recommend. I'm afraid I can't be much help.

Howard, you can be a *big* help. I'd like to use your name as a personal reference. We worked closely together on last year's school budget campaign, and I was impressed by your energy, your effectiveness, and your ability to communicate. I hoped your observations of me were equally good, and that you wouldn't mind saying so in a letter.

I'm honored to be asked! I couldn't have done all I did without your assistance in supplying the numbers to support our arguments. Talk about analytical skill! The Board of Ed is still talking about the accuracy of your projections.

If you'd put those thoughts into a short letter for me, I'd be most appreciative. With your power of expression, I can't lose.

I'd be delighted. I'll have my secretary type it tomorrow, and I'll drop it off on my way home.

Thanks. Please stop in for a cup of coffee, if you can. I have a copy of my resume to give you, and a list of questions a caller might ask you. I'd also like to catch up on construction progress at the new school.

Sounds good. I should be there around six. And Betty, in the meantime, please ask Frank what he's feeding those roses!

Okay, so it might not be that easy. And, perhaps you haven't earned your CPA or don't have a neighbor whose letterhead tilts from too much type. Fortunately, you don't need those things.

If you look at your life, you will be gratified to see just how many respectful and respectable friends and acquaintances will help you. That respect will be nurtured even further by your humble, honest, hopeful request; by their appreciation at being asked and being able to help; and by the way you impress them with doing your homework.

OVERCOMING OBJECTIONS

When asking for a personal reference, the most common objections you will face, even from your closest friends, are:

I've never given a reference before.

I'm not sure how to go about it.

I'm afraid I'll say something wrong.

I'm no good at writing letters.

To overcome the first three objections, reassure your references that you have prepared a small package of materials—a sample application, your resume, and a list of questions typically asked; you will go over the key points you'd like them to cover; and you are sure that, if they just review everything carefully and respond naturally, the questioner will be very impressed.

To references who don't write well, reply that you have several brief, effective letter styles already drafted, and you'll be happy to give them copies, help draft the letter, and if necessary, have it typed. If you know these people well enough, just ask for their letterhead and knock yourself out. Their autographs on the signature line is all you need. Be sure to give them a copy so they know what they wrote.

To all reluctant references, express the importance of their help and how much you appreciate it. If they're still hesitant, perhaps you misjudged the relationship. There are plenty of others on your list. Pick an alternate. The genuine enthusiasm of your references is crucial to your success.

PREPARING YOUR REFERENCES

So, now you have called your top five names and numbers (with a few backups for unavailable or uncooperative ones). Next, you must prepare them to focus on the character traits, background, and skills you want prospective employers to see.

Send or give the five people a copy of the list of questions they will be asked in a telephone call (Chapter 5), a sample of a letter you'd like them to write (Chapter 6), and a copy of your high-class resume. Sit down with each (if possible), or call and go over at some length the kind of position you are targeting, the skills and abilities the employer seeks, and what it is you think they can say to make your success more likely. Also, in *How to Turn an Interview into a Job*, I advised, "Ask them to accept the telephone call or return it immediately (offering to pay any toll charges), and to notify you of the details the moment they hang up. You need the feedback and you need it *fast*. At the very least, you will have presented some good character witnesses to help your case."[2]

But the very least will be the very best if your references impress the interviewer with their credentials, personality, sincerity, and enthusiasm in recommending you. A job offer will probably be generated.

Chapter

4

Perfect Professional Telephone References

If you've ever done reference checking, you know that most of the time professional references are *anything* but professional. It's not apparent, but it's understandable. They are invariably caught off guard during a busy day. They haven't been prepared—or even notified—by the person who gave his or her name as a reference, and they don't clearly recall the highlights of that person's career at their company. (Sorry—you're not any exception to the rule. In your job, you're only as good as your last [fill in the blank]).

Your professional telephone references will be different, though. You selected the top four to six colleagues from your professional past (or present). Then, you reached out to them, renewed the relationships, and revived their positive experiences with you.

Your phone calls served as an "audition" for the best announcers to advertise you. Then you selected the best ones. Next, you're going to meet with them (or talk at length on the telephone, in the case of faraway references), give them their scripts, and rehearse them into an award-winning performance.

YOUR PROFESSIONAL REFERENCE PREPARATION PACKAGE

You need four things to give (or send) to each one of your references:

- A sample completed application.

- Your resume.
- Your individualized "reference summary."
- The Professional Reference Questions list.

Read on . . .

Your Resume

This book is not about resumes; nonetheless, you will need a good one. You should take the time to write an updated, interesting, impressive resume for your current job search.

Since many books have been written about resumes, there's a lot of information on the shelves. A lot of misinformation, too. Here's my fail-safe advice for the only resume that counts—a *hiresume*—one that gets you hired.

Your "Hiresume" Should:

1. Be only one page long.

This is the most difficult and most important part of resume preparation. It's a direct-mail advertising piece, not an autobiography. Please don't fight that difference. Refine it by crossing out words, rewriting phrases, and focusing your job years in a streamlined career path. Even if you never use that resume, the self-discipline of refining it is the best interviewing exercise in the job gym.

Use generalized, action-oriented phrases like these to get the interviewer going:

"Consistently performed . . ."
"Developed a series of . . ."
"Organized several . . ."

"Was promoted to progressively responsible positions in . . ."

"Was responsible for a number of . . ."

2. Be typed in 12-pitch (or larger) size if typed, or typeset in 10-point fonts.

A few different typefaces, occasional boldface, and thoughtful underlining will keep the hirer awake. But don't use more than three of each. Consistent favorites are Times Roman type if typeset, or Courier if typed (with carbon ribbon). These sizes and styles are readable, available, and acceptable.

3. Be printed with black ink on white paper.

Off-white stock can be equally effective. The paper weight should be at least 24-pound. The effect of colors is unpredictable, but almost all photocopiers are allergic to at least one. You want that resume to be foremost and forwarded.

Jobseekers don't understand the importance of conservatism. Staff employees who hire aren't risk-takers. They want dependable, manageable, serious workers. Black ink on white paper. Nice.

4. Have at least a one-inch border.

A border not only frames the resume, but over 80 percent of the people reviewing it will write in the margins. If a cover sheet must be completed and stapled to it, that resume loses its impulse impact.

5. Include your name, address, and telephone number centered at the top.

Make it easy to call you. If your address and numbers are

at the bottom, they might be overlooked. After a few sloppy copies, they might not even be there.

6. Include a few select items of personal data.

Credentials are like optional equipment. Job-related affiliations are like warranties. Just leave off any reference to religion, race, politics, or anything that's controversial.

7. Summarize your experience, beginning with your most recent position.

This part of your resume can be presented in several acceptable ways. It's helpful to work backward from the kinds of positions you want to focus on the areas of emphasis. Listing or summarizing similar responsibilities is appropriate, but you must be concise. This is known as the "chronological" resume.

Some authorities advise a more generalized, "functional" resume for people who have changed jobs more than every two years. Unfortunately, it is almost impossible to write in generalities without looking like you're hiding something. Interviewers don't trust functional resumes—they know the game. So write chronologically, combining and omitting job hops.

Your "Hiresume" Should Not:

1. Be updated or underlined in handwriting.

Highlighting should either be done when the resume is prepared, or not at all. Updating addresses and positions in handwriting stops that resume cold. Even if a hiring authority says it doesn't matter, it does. To him or her or someone else. Since the resume is *you* at this point, make sure it has class.

2. Contain details about references.

Here is everything you need and want: "Personal and professional references are available. They will be furnished upon request, once mutual interest has been established."

You are not about to reveal those super-references until you know who'll call them, when, and what they want to hear. Besides, the last thing you want is for them to be overrehearsed. They'll sound too canned and disinterested.

3. Indicate a salary amount.

What you received in former jobs is irrelevant. In fact, voluntarily disclosing it should be illegal—you're invading your own privacy.

Knowing your "requirement" is valuable to a prospective employer, so it can screen you out. It works, too—the probability of your "requirement" being too high or too low is statistically 100 percent.

When Sent to a Personnel Department, Your "Hiresume" Should Not:

1. State your target job.

If you know the job being offered and you don't care about being considered for anything else, fine. Useless, but fine. You think you're aiming at a target job, but you'd better buy a pair of bulletproof wingtips.

2. Be introduced by a cover letter.

As with a salary objective, a cover letter can be counterproductive, pointing you away from the target job. Unless you *really* know something about it, or want to identify your referral, lose your prose. Overworked personnelers will—along with your resume.

However, if you are aiming at a known supervisor who *really* knows what he or she wants, a well-drafted cover letter can be effective. Most supervisors don't. Even if this one does, he or she won't route your resume anywhere else.

Write and produce your high-class resume *before* you begin to contact your references. It's part of the kit you'll give them.

The Reference Summary

Most professional references are less interested in reading resumes than overworked personnel staffers. They want sales training, not reading lessons. That means "sizzle"—"closers" in the form of inspirational, motivational, believable experiences with you.

Your homework includes a brief, neatly typed, one-page summary (preferably with short headings) that reviews the significant facts in your references' eyewitness testimony. Concentrate on traits, skills, and accomplishments that apply to target jobs. See, for example, the sample reference summary on the next page.

Be honest, but not modest. Modesty in references telegraphs uncertainty, concealment, and even misrepresentation. Few references will overstate beyond your data, but many will understate. So give them every syllable you want them to utter. Do it right, and you might even get a call like this:

Hey, John, I got this list you sent me. What's wrong with you? You didn't say anything about the increased system sales and the time you won the national sales award!

Prepare a summary for each reference, and keep a copy for *your* reference during your interviews.

Sample Reference Summary

Name: *John R. Smith*   Telephone No.: *(917)321-8732*

Former Title: *National Sales Manager*

ACCOMPLISHMENTS

- Supervised and motivated a field sales force that grew from 12 people to 20 during three-year tenure. Managed and led in-house sales support staff of six.

- Set and monitored sales objectives by territory and product, resulting in an average annual increase in sales of 30 percent, with an overall three-year cumulative increase of 120 percent (from $6 million in 1980 to $13.2 million in 1983).

- Purchased and installed computerized sales monitoring and reporting system.

- Used customer feedback to help create and market three new products, the Accu Soft, the Accu Sort, and the Accu Scan, which are consistently among the top sellers produced by the company.

- Established a sales incentive program that increased sales across the board, and more than 50 percent each in the two lowest performing territories.

TRAITS:

- Fast-moving, effective, results-oriented.
- Highly skilled at motivating others to achieve their goals.
- Reliable, loyal, enthusiastic.

The Professional Reference Questions List

The third item you will give each reference is two versions of a list of questions they are likely to be asked in a telephone reference check. The first will have "suggested" answers completed by you. This helps them "remember." (Your secret's safe with me.) Perhaps they never knew you when you worked together or what you did. No matter. What's wrong with a little help to help helpers help? They're not on trial—you are. And they're not under oath. Act too technical about this, and you might as well call some stranger and say, "I couldn't stand working with you and wouldn't ask you for a reference anyway."

Give each of your references a copy of the blank list, so they can use the completed one and other data to answer the questions in their own words. They won't, but it shows respect.

Professional Reference Questions

How long have you known _____ ?

How do you know _____ ?

When was he/she hired? _____

When did he/she leave? _____

What was his/her salary when he/she left?_____

Why did he/she leave? _____

Did you work with him/her directly? _____

Was he/she usually on time? _____

Was he/she absent from work very often? _____

Did his/her personal life ever interfere with his/her work? _____

What were his/her titles? _____

What were his/her duties? _____

Did he/she cooperate with supervisors? _____

Did he/she cooperate with coworkers? _____

Did he/she take work home very often?_____

What are his/her primary attributes? _____

_____

What are his/her primary liabilities? _____

Is he/she eligible for rehire? _____

Can you confirm the information he/she has given? _____

Of course, review any sensitive areas. If you were going through a divorce when you worked with your reference, and he or she remembers that your personal life interfered with your work (whose doesn't?), don't leave his or her response to chance. Say something like:

> **I know I was going through some rough times during that period. I wouldn't have made it without your support. How will you answer questions about my attendance and productivity?**

Need I tell you the answer? Confront a ghost and it vanishes. Fear it, and it haunts your hunt. People don't tell the truth, even if they want to. They tell their *perception* of the truth.

OVERCOMING OBJECTIONS

If a reference plainly objects to something you wrote in your preparation materials, or has a different memory of the past, listen carefully and make changes. It's rare, but you might hear:

I don't know about this computerized sales reporting system you say you installed. I know you were involved, but the controller was really responsible. Could we just say you *participated* in choosing and installing a system?

(Your gracious reply, with a smile:)

Of course. Your way really is more accurate, but it still sounds good. That's fine.

Then review the process, summarize the key points, and tell your references you will notify them of who will be calling, when, and why.

FOLLOW-UP TO A PHOTO FINISH

Communicate with your references throughout your job search. Don't call without a reason, but make brief, time-conscious telephone contacts to inquire if they received the expected calls, how the conversations went, and if they will be available for future inquiries. You don't want to give the name of a reference who won't be there. If one is traveling on business, ask if he or she will be checking in with the office for messages and returning the calls before he or she returns.

CONSIDER THEM LIFETIME LIFELINES

Most of all, don't forget your references once they have helped you get the job. Let them be the second to know. Express your appreciation in a phone call or letter, and promptly send a thank-you gift. Be sure they know you will be there for them when they need you, too. If you haven't been an effective professional networker in the past, start now.

The best PR for you is Personal References and Professional References. Your career campaign shouldn't end until you retire.

Chapter

5

Perfect Personal Telephone References

The technique to develop perfect personal telephone references is similar to the technique for developing professional ones. The two essential elements are the reference's *credibility* and *knowledge* about you. Follow the steps in this chapter and success will be yours.

You screened your personal references when you asked them for their help. From their responses, you determined who was most presentable and who would give the best presentation. Now you must give your personal references the information they need to come through for you. Every personal reference needs to know how to present a profile of you, the applicant, that fits the employer's "wish list."

YOUR PERSONAL REFERENCE PREPARATION PACKAGE

Your personal references will need the following items:

- Your resume.
- Your reference summary.
- The Personal Reference Questions list.

Your Resume

Review Chapter 4 for suggestions to help you prepare a "hire-sume." The purpose of giving it to your personal references, even if they have never been involved with you professionally, is to provide them with an overview. This includes what you do as well as insight into your profession or industry. The description of your work, complete with the buzzwords in your field, will help prepare them for the reference-check call.

The Reference Summary

Next, give each reference a one-page summary, or list, describing attributes and activities that:

> 1. The reference can authenticate;
>
>   and
>
> 2. Are relevant to your target job.

Remember Betty Brown, the CPA from Chapter 3, and Howard, her personal reference? Howard knew Betty as a neighbor and as a fellow community volunteer when they campaigned together for a school budget increase. Howard's personal experiences with Betty can reveal the character traits *and* job skills he has observed, as outlined in the summary on the next page.

Prepare a similar summary to review with your references. This is the "wish-fulfillment list" that matches the prospective employer's wish list for the position you want. Be sure the references understand and agree with the contents.

Don't be embarrassed about selling yourself too much. You can't—your references need as much coaching as possible. Most will be grateful to be liberated from the task of describing you. They will be glad to have the adjectives and verbs on the summary when the reference checker calls.

As you review the individualized summary with each reference, be sure he or she understands:

- The objectives of your job search.

Sample Reference Summary

Name: *Betty R. Brown*   Telephone No.: *(616) 522-3359*

Position Desired: *Accountant, Insurance Company*

CHARACTER TRAITS

- Determination
- Accuracy
- Thoroughness
- Commitment
- Follow-through
- Energy
- Enthusiasm
- Competence
- Positive attitude

JOB-RELATED ABILITIES AND SKILLS:

- Compiled financial data and developed complete, accurate forecasts.
- Presented concise, understandable financial reports for budget projections.
- Demonstrated knowledge of accounting principles and procedures.

- The specific knowledge that you'd like him or her to relate in a reference call.

- The delivery necessary for maximum impact on the reference checker.

The summary may vary slightly if you are targeting more than one type of job. In that case, you may give each reference two or more summaries, each titled appropriately.

It is desirable for each list to be slightly different from the others. If you coach your references too well, and they are all using identical language, their recommendations will appear canned. The impact of spontaneity, candor, and credibility is lost.

The Personal Reference Questions List

The final item to give each reference is a duplicate list of questions they are likely to be asked by a reference checker. The first copy should have "suggested" answers written by you.

This list is designed to be helpful, to refresh your references' memory about dates and details of your relationship, and to make sure that what *you* say is verified by what your *references* say. It is the final step in the subtle, careful coaching process that prepares your eyewitness references to testify accurately and consistently to the facts you presented.

The second copy of the list you provide should be blank, without answers, to allow your references to use the information you have given them and their own recall to create their versions of their visions.

Personal Reference Questions

How long have you known _____ ?

How do you know _____ ?

What is your opinion of _____ ?

Does (he/she) get along well with others?_____

Is (he/she) usually on time?_____

Is (he/she) absent from work very often?_____

Does (he/she) bring work home very often?_____

Does (he/she) like (his/her) job?_____

What are (his/her) primary attributes?_____

_____

What are (his/her) primary liabilities? _____

_____

TROUBLE-SHOOTING

What is said to the reference checker is too important to be left unsaid by you. Even well-meaning references can reply inappropriately when they're unprepared.

Look carefully at the list. It contains loaded questions: *Is (he/she) easy to get along with? What are (his/her) primary liabilities?* Your coaching should prepare your references to be ready with a highly developed reply.

The completed reference summary prepared your references to discuss your "attributes." You can help them handle the question about liabilities equally well. Here are some answers that can transform liabilities into assets:

Well, the one liability that comes to mind is that (he/she) considers (himself/herself) last. (He's/She's) never too busy to help someone or volunteer for another position. (He's/She's) one of those people who proves the truth of the phrase, "If you want it done, give it to a busy person."

It's funny, though. (He/She) never seems to get ruffled about it all. (He's/She's) organized, efficient, and goal-oriented. It seems that the more (he/she) does, the happier (he/she) is.

(His/her) liabilities? Oh, I guess you could say (he's/she's) a workaholic! (He's/She's) canceled our Saturday morning tennis game on several occasions because (he/she) wanted to work on (his/her) projects while the office was quiet. Completing (his/her) work has consistently been (his/her) top priority. (He's/She's) very dedicated.

Always end a discussion of a liability or weakness by turning it into an *attribute* or *strength*.

"Is (he/she) easy to get along with?" can be a loaded question. Someone can be too "easy" if he or she is unable to say "No." In this case, the answer would be:

(He/She) is firm, but fair. I've never seen (him/her) arbitrary; instead, (he/she) sets reasonable rules and expects them to be upheld. I've always found (him/her) very likable and concerned about the welfare of others, but (he/she) is no pushover.

WHAT TO EXPECT

Most reference checkers will introduce themselves with their name, their company, your name, and the position you're seeking. The words almost always sound like:

Hello, Mr. Smith. I'm Harry Anderson from XYZ Manufacturing, and I'm calling with regard to Darryl Tompkins, who has applied for the position of Cost Control Manager with our company. He gave your name as a personal reference. Can you tell me . . .

If the caller does not identify the kind of job, instruct your references to ask politely, "Can you tell me what position _____ has applied for?" This will serve to cue them about the nature of the job and which items from your reference summary (or which of several summaries you have provided) to accentuate.

Stay close to your references throughout your search, and alert them to the kinds of jobs you are seeking. When one employer's "wish list" varies slightly from another's (and you know you have enough qualities to fill both lists), call your references and advise them which traits and skills to emphasize to which reference checkers.

REHEARSE FOR A STAR PERFORMANCE

Prepare sample answers like those given here, and rehearse the "script" with your references. Don't let pride or hope cause you to ignore this essential, critical step in the coaching phase. You are the director and producer, and what your actors *say* and *convey* is your responsibility. Do your job well, and you will be accepting the Academy Award—in the form of a new job.

The "actor factor" operates exactly as I discussed in *The Complete Q&A Job Interview Book*:

> There are only so many questions that can be asked, and only so many ways to ask them. Oh, there might be minor variations—like the accent of the interviewer, his or her tone of voice, or a pause here and there. Experienced jobgetters appreciate them. Otherwise, they'd undoubtedly start snoring before the offers were extended.
>
> Since interviews are so predictable, they're *controllable*. Only the places and faces change—not the words. And you can have them all embedded in your subconscious, ready for instant replay at the drop of an interesting job lead.

I know. You think "background," "qualifications," or "experience" have something to do with getting hired. You're right—not about the *job*, though. About *interviewing*! The director only knows what you show. That's why the actor factor is so "critical."[1]

These are your friends, remember! Arrange for enough time to explain your objectives, and show your references how they can help you achieve them. Meet personally over a quiet lunch or dinner (your treat, of course), and let them know how important this is to you. Give them your carefully prepared information and go over it in detail.

Resist the temptation to give in when a personal reference says:

Hey, I don't need your resume or any of this paperwork. I'll just tell them a bunch of lies. Don't worry. You'll sound great!

Explain that it is important to you to sound great with the *facts*, and only those closest to you know just how to express them.

FOLLOW-UP

Ask your references to accept the telephone calls or return them immediately (offering to pay any toll charges), and to notify you of the details the moment they hang up. You need the feedback and you need it *fast*.

When it's all over, and you're sitting in that fancy new office, remember to call all those people who "knew you when" to let them know you "remember them *now*."

Chapter

6

Elements of a Perfect Reference Letter

The "letter of introduction" used to be a business prerequisite. A letter written to one influential person by another on your behalf could get you an interview and, practically, a job.

That letter of introduction was really a reference letter testifying to your honesty, integrity, and worthiness for the job. The recommendation of an important person gave you a receptive, interested, motivated hiring audience.

As our culture changed, the letter of introduction became almost extinct. The Industrial Revolution meant mass production, mass marketing, and—ultimately—mass mailed resumes. But almost no jobs are filled by mass hiring. They're filled one by one in that highly personal, subjective, unscientific activity we call the hiring process.

RETURN OF THE REFERENCE LETTER

You've probably been advised not to attach a reference letter to your resume, or to give the names of your references until after the interview and when a job offer is likely. That's because most jobseekers use the wrong *kind* of reference letter, and use it the wrong *way*. Let's rewrite the standard one so it will supercharge your search and generate your job.

71

Do's, Don'ts, Wills, and Won'ts

As I said in Chapter 3, don't attach a reference letter to a resume going to the personnel department. Personnelers are too busy to read them; and, even if they do, the name of the writer and the gist of the contents are probably meaningless. At best, you've wasted the paper. At worst, you've wasted the interview.

Then there's the matter of the reference letter itself. Forget about the general "to-whom-it-may-concern" variety. You know—the kind that's been photocopied so many times it's hardly readable. The less readable, the better. It was probably written years ago by someone who hardly even remembers your *name*!

If read at all, the letter just creates doubt about your credibility. In some cases, it even contains wording inconsistent from your resume.

Third-Party Power

What *will* launch you to fame and fortune is a super-reference, *written by* the right person, *targeted to* the right person (a decision-maker), and containing marketable information about your abilities and skills. What someone else says about you has ten times the influence of what you say about yourself.

Use a brief, perfectly drafted one-page letter—from a carefully selected reference—as a *cover letter* for your resume. Personalize each letter to individuals inside the target company(ies) who either have:

- The authority to hire you,

  or

- Connections to those who do.

POSITION POWER

Marketeers always think about *positioning* a product or service. You have a service (your skills) and a product (you) to sell. To position you into the perfect position, you must position them correctly. It's nothing more than positioning yourself for the perfect position.

What are the ingredients of a positioning letter? The letter should position its writer as an authority, be directed to the person with the proper position within the proper company, and be written to position you as an indispensable product with an incredible service.

Presto!

WHO TO SELECT

Selection of the reference cover-letter writer is the first element of positioning. He or she should be:

- Someone who knows the recipient of the letter.
- Someone who knows someone else the recipient knows.
- Someone who, by reputation, is known to the recipient of the letter.
- Someone whose letterhead, title, and responsibilities will attract the recipient's attention or give credibility to the statements in the letter—and to you.

The writer of the reference cover letter should hold an equal or superior position to the recipient. An exception might be when the letter is written from a former employee who left in good standing and has a cordial relationship with his or her former boss. Another exception might be when the reference is on good terms with a higher level executive from another company whom he or she met at a conference or while serving on a committee.

Increase Your Know-Who Know-How

Targeting the letter is the second essential element of positioning. When you contacted all your references, you advertised your availability. Many will have said, "Gee, I know ————, who's in charge of manufacturing (accounting/customer service/management information systems) at ———— company. Maybe I can put you in touch with him."

Never refuse an offer like that. If your references don't offer, ask. Even if none can give you a push or a pull, perhaps they know someone who can.

Consider the case of "Judy," who knew how to generate respectable reference representation:

> Judy was stalled in her job as a writer of programming manuals for a small East Coast software manufacturer. She had been with the company for three years and had been promoted to supervisor of her department of four writers and a technical editor.
>
> Although her undergraduate degree was in computer science, she studied at night to complete an MBA with an emphasis in marketing. Judy believed that her education, combined with her knowledge of user needs, prepared her for a marketing manager position. But her company had only one such position, and it didn't look like it would be vacant soon.
>
> So, Judy decided to review her contacts to find a few superstars who could become super-references. She

wanted them to supercharge her into a bigger company where she could maximize her marketing training.

She decided on:

"Judd," a former coworker, who left to start a small software company. Although Judd's company only had a few products, one of them had recently been successful and was getting loads of industry attention. Judd's letterhead read "Justin Davis, President, Specialized Software Corporation" with a prestigious Los Angeles address.

Then there was "Elizabeth," a marketing manager of computer peripherals whom Judy had met at a conference; and

"Dr. William Dutton," an adjunct faculty member at the graduate school of business where Judy had studied, a former government official, and the director of competitive intelligence for a defense manufacturing company. Judy took Dr. Dutton's course in competitive intelligence and business marketing. They became friends and she even helped him prepare a manuscript.

Judy's three principal references had a wealth of contacts in the software marketing business who could help her target marketing directors of manufacturers. The letters they wrote to introduce her and direct attention to her resume won her interview after interview. She had four reference-influenced offers, and today she's rapidly climbing the marketing ladder at one of the world's biggest software manufacturers.

Your story can be just that simple, its ending just that sweet. Even if you don't know any highly placed officials or company presidents, *somewhere* among your professional and personal contacts is *someone* (and another, and another) who will write a credible cover letter to get your resume read, your interview set, and your job offered.

Style and Substance

The third critical element of positioning is the letter's contents. This is your sales copy, the words that will intrigue, persuade, and motivate your reader. In look and "hook," the letter should be a superseller.

Now, let's review the mechanical, or physical, elements of the letter—its style. Then we'll discuss its substance.

THE BETTER LETTER LOOK

In *The Perfect Cover Letter*, Richard Beatty discussed letter forms in detail, and told how to create the right "look" for your cover letter:

> The physical layout and design of a cover letter are important to its effectiveness for several reasons.
>
> First, good layout and design enhance appearance and serve to create a favorable impression on the part of the reader. A letter that is well designed, properly spaced, and neat will create a positive image of you as an individual. It will suggest to prospective employers that you are logical, neat, and well organized. Conversely, an improperly or poorly designed letter can convey just the opposite and thus leave a negative impression.
>
> Second, a neat, concise, and well-organized format will substantially improve readability and thereby enhance communications and increase the probability that your cover letter will be read. Additionally, a good format will properly highlight the important aspects of your credentials, thus improving the chances of successfully marketing yourself to prospective employers.

Third, failure to employ an acceptable business letter format may suggest that you are ignorant of common business practices or, worse, that you simply don't care. Neither impression will help your cause and may, in fact, detract substantially from your self-marketing efforts and your overall job hunting plan.[1]

These principles apply equally to the effectiveness of reference cover letters. In fact, they are the same for all serious business correspondence. It is more than a "cover"—it's a package. It's a preview of what's inside. You're either ready to buy it, or you're not.

Rules for Cover Letter Style

Cover letters should be:

1. Originals, not photocopies, signed in black ink.

2. No more than one page long.

3. Typed, on a self-correcting typewriter (or word processor) with a carbon ribbon, in 12-pitch type with margins no longer than 10 and 70.

4. Fully addressed with no abbreviations, containing the middle initial and title of the recipient.

5. Free from errors or erasures. ("White-out" is out, too.)

6. On high quality (personal or professional) letterhead.

7. No more than four paragraphs:

   a. The *introductory paragraph*, wherein the writer introduces himself or herself and mentions briefly how he/she knows you.

   b. The *value paragraph*, which describes the applicant's background and highlights his or her key abilities that will benefit the target company. Although it's the longest paragraph of the letter, it should *not* be more than five or six sentences. It *should* be both sincere and persuasive.

  c. The *action paragraph*, which asks the reader to read the resume enclosed and contact the applicant for an interview (or wait patiently for him or her to call).

  d. A *closing paragraph*, which expresses appreciation.

That's all you need to know about formatting the letter. Chapter 7 gives you samples of good reference cover letters. Review them for the specific words to use.

Content

The letter should have an interesting, upbeat style, while remaining businesslike. If the reference knows the target personally, it can be slightly less formal.

The language should be persuasive. The writer should be enthusiastic about recommending you. The content should focus on its main point—getting you an interview and consideration for a job. Every word should either "frame" or state that message.

There should be no run-on sentences or long paragraphs. Key points in italic or boldface type are appropriate if limited to no more than a *total* of five.

HOW TO HELP YOUR REFERENCES WRITE BETTER LETTERS

You really can't—they don't have a clue about what to do. That's why typical reference letters are ridiculous.

References aren't particularly good learners, either. After all, if they weren't more important than you, you wouldn't need them to lend you their importance, right? It's not only *their* belief—it's yours. So, rather than try to teach them or leave the letters' impact to chance, *write them yourself!*

I have clients do this in court pleadings all the time. They know the facts far better than I ever will because they *lived* them. The result is a far more detailed, consistent presentation. Just ask your reference. You'll probably hear:

Sure, whatever you want. Just type it up and I'll sign it.

At the very least, if the reference wants to take full responsibility for drafting and producing the letter, you can give him or her a copy of the "Rules for Cover Letter Style," presented earlier in this chapter, and ask him or her to follow them as closely as possible.

If the reference is a personal friend or colleague well known to the target, the opening and closing paragraphs should be in the writer's own words. But you can help by supplying the language for the value paragraph.

Use your judgment. The key is finding the right reference to aim you straight at the right target job. After that, the letter formatting is a routine process. Chapter 7 provides a crash course on it.

Chapter

7

Examples of Perfect Reference Letters

All effective reference letters have three features in common. They are:

- Upbeat.
- Concise.
- Direct.

These balanced, believable "better letters" will bring you offer after offer. Even if writing isn't your strength, the examples that follow will help you develop a proven approach to communication and motivation in writing.

Certain techniques work; the rest don't. It's not a matter of *preference*, but of *proof*. If it works, it's here. If it doesn't, it's not. The further you deviate from the perfect pattern and prose, the less likely it is that the letter will work for you.

BLOCK FORMAT TO WIN

Since the reference cover letter is a *business* letter (with personal information), Beatty recommended in *The Perfect Cover Letter* that the block format be used.[1] Therefore, the examples that follow are written in simple, accepted block style. Its features are:

- Indented return address and date.
- Spaces between paragraphs.
- Double-indented complimentary closing.
- Triple-indented signature line.

Block Letter Format

```
                    (return address)    XXXXXXXXXXXXXXX
                                        XXXXXXXXXXXXXXX

                            (date)      XXXXXXXXXXXXXX

XXXXXXXXXXXXXXXXXXX (address)
XXXXXXXXXXXXXXXXXX
XXXXXXXXXXXXXXXXXX

Re: XXXXXXXXXXXXXXXXXXXXXXXXX

XXXXXXXXXXXXXXXXXX (salutation)

XXXXXXXXXXXXXXXXXXXXXXXXXXXXXXXXXXXXXXXXXXXXXXXXXXXXXXXXXX
XXXXXXXXXXXXXXXXXXXXXXXXXXXXXXXXXXXXXXXXXXXXXXXXXXXXXXXXXX
XXXXXXXXXXXXXXXXXXXXXXXXXXXXXXXXXXXXXXXXXXXXXXXXXXXXXXXXXX
XXXXXXXXXXXXXXXXXXXXXXXXXXXXXXXXXXXXXXXXXXXXXXXXXXXXXXXXXX

XXXXXXXXXXXXXXXXXXXXXXXXXXXXXXXXXXXXXXXXXXXXXXXXXXXXXXXXXX
XXXXXXXXXXXXXXXXXXXXXXXXXXXXXXXXXXXXXXXXXXXXXXXXXXXXXXXXXX
XXXXXXXXXXXXXXXXXXXXXXXXXXXXXXXXXXXXXXXXXXXXXXXXXXXXXXXXXX
XXXXXXXXXXXXXXXXXXXXXXXXXXXXXXXXXXXXXXXXXXXXXXXXXXXXXXXXXX
XXXXXXXXXXXXXXXXXXXXXXXXXXXXXXXXXXXXXXXXXXXXXXXXXXXXXXXXXX
XXXXXXXXXXXXXXXXXXXXXXXXXXXXXXXXXXXXXXXXXXXXXXXXXXXXXXXXXX

XXXXXXXXXXXXXXXXXXXXXXXXXXXXXXXXXXXXXXXXXXXXXXXXXXXXXXXXXX
XXXXXXXXXXXXXXXXXXXXXXXXXXXXXXXXXXXXXXXXXXXXXXXXXXXXXXXXXX
XXXXXXXXXXXXXXXXXXXXXXXXXXXXXXXXXXXXXXXXXXXXXXXXXXXXXXXXXX
XXXXXXXXXXXXXXXXXXXXXXXXXXXXXXXXXXXXXXXXXXXXXXXXXXXXXXXXXX

XXXXXXXXXXXXXXXXXXXXXXXXXXXXXXXXXXXXXXXXXXXXXXXXXXXXXXXXXX
XXXXXXXXXXXXXXXXXXXXXXXXXXXXXXXXXXXXXXXXXXXXXXXXXXXXXXXXXX
XXXXXXXXXXXXXXXXXXXXXXXXXXXXXXXXXXXXXXXXXXXXXXXXXXXXXXXXXX

            (complimentary closing)     XXXXXXXXXXXXXXX


                    (signature line)    XXXXXXXXXXXXXXX

XXX:xxx      (typist identification)
XXXXXXXXXXX (enclosure line)
```

Study the examples that follow and imitate (or copy) their approach. Your secret's safe with me. Note that each sample is interesting and readable. There are short, crisp sentences and concise paragraphs. Each thought bridges logically to the next. In a word, the letters *move!*

PRACTICE MAKES PERFECT

To make your reference letters perfect, practice! Draft a few, then read them aloud—to yourself and others. If they don't pass the read-aloud test for clarity and interest, rewrite them. The effort to make them powerful will open doors you literally didn't know existed.

Perfect Reference Letter Example 1

In this situation, the reference never met the target personally, but heard him speak at a conference. This provided a perfect chance to compliment him while establishing credibility and "mutuality" in the opening paragraph. Furthermore, the reference's letterhead reveals he has an important position—at least one level up from the target's—in a well-known company.

Perfect Reference Letter Example 2

Here the reference is not personally acquainted with the target, but his letterhead overcomes this minor technicality. As a presiding judge and a former employer of the young attorney, that letter and her resume will be read—receptively.

Perfect Reference Letter Example 3

In this sample letter, the reference and the target enjoy a warm, long-lived professional relationship. The tone is warmer, more personal. This allows the writer to be more insistent and more urgent.

Example 1

MONOLITH MANUFACTURING, INCORPORATED
4382 Industrial Boulevard
Des Moines, Iowa 50309
(515) 384-2900

Jared L. Alexander
Director of Operations
Recreation Products Division

January 10, 19__

Matthew Austin, Manager
Traffic Department
Allied Manufacturing
225 Atlantic Avenue
Shalimar, Florida 32200

Re: Jason D. Scott Reference

Dear Mr. Austin:

I thoroughly enjoyed your presentation at the National
Traffic Managers Conference last month in Dallas. As soon
as I returned to my office, I called a meeting of the
Monolith transportation managers and began at once
implementing your innovative cost-control recommendations.
They're already working!

I'd like to refer Jason Scott to you. Jason is an
outstanding traffic manager with more than 15 years
experience in operations. He has moved over $100 million a
year in goods and is seeking a position with Allied.

I give Jason an unqualified endorsement. As his enclosed
resume reveals, his experience ranges from moving raw
materials to finished goods in a variety of industrial
settings. I met Jason when we worked together at General
International. Within six months he reorganized the entire
traffic department there, cut the carrier list from 35 to
15, and greatly reduced paperwork.

Fortunately, Jason is available now when you're looking for
a traffic manager for your chemicals operation. I don't
know anyone who could do a better job than Jason Scott.
He'll be calling you next week to discuss meeting with you.

Best wishes for continued success!

Sincerely,

Jared L. Alexander

JLA:bes
Enclosure: Jason D. Scott Resume

Example 2

The Honorable Milton A. Handel
Judge of the Superior Court
State of Massachusetts
100 Commonwealth Avenue
Boston, Massachusetts 02203

February 6, 19__

Christopher Ryan, Esq.
Ryan, Douglas & Brandeis, P.C.
2500 John Hancock Building
Boston, Massachusetts 02214

Re: Elizabeth M. Morgan Reference

Dear Mr. Ryan:

I am pleased to refer Elizabeth Morgan to you for
consideration as an associate with Ryan, Douglas, &
Brandeis.

As you will note from the enclosed resume, Elizabeth not
only graduated with honors but served as a Contributing
Editor of the University of Massachusetts Law Review.

Elizabeth worked as a legal assistant at Handel and
Silverberg, P.C., during two years that I was the Senior
Partner. When I was appointed to the bench, she entered the
University of Massachusetts Law School. Elizabeth performed
her duties with the utmost professionalism and dedication.
She had responsibility for our consumer litigation files,
which she managed with exceptional results. I have followed
Elizabeth's three years in law school closely, and I am
pleased (but not surprised) that she has distinguished
herself there as well.

At a time when law school graduates seem to lack a
commitment to excellence, Elizabeth is an outstanding
exception. I would appreciate it if you would give her
qualifications serious consideration. She will call you
directly for an interview within the next few weeks.

Sincerely,

Milton A. Handel

MAH:lfp

Enclosure: Elizabeth M. Morgan Resume

Example 3

TPT

Thompson Professional Temporaries
100 Executive Plaza, Suite 17
Raleigh, North Carolina 27609

March 20, 19__

John T. MacDonald, C.P.A.
MacDonald and Dennis, P.C.
125 Prospect Street
New Hope, North Carolina 27604

Re: Donald J. Black Reference

Dear John:

Too many months have passed since we've talked. I intend to
call you to meet for lunch as soon as tax season is over.

I know how busy you are this time of year, but there's
someone else you should meet, too. Late last year, a bright
young man named Donald Black worked as a temp accountant
for several months. At the time, Don was studying for his
C.P.A. exam. In spite of this, he filled temp assignments
for us, performing them all extremely well. Our clients
were most impressed by his adaptability to a new business.
In less than a day, he is able to understand detailed
accounting procedures.

As you will see from the resume I've enclosed, Don passed
the certification exam with one of the highest scores on
record. He has asked me to recommend him for a position
with your firm, and I am doing so with pleasure. We'd like
to keep him on our payroll, but this young man is going
places.

I can't think of a better place than MacDonald and Dennis!
Don will call you in a week or so for an interview. I hope
you'll seize this chance in spite of your hectic schedule.
Opportunity knocks!

By the way, our next lunch is on me.

                              Best regards,

                              Julia N. Thompson

JNT:rms
Enclosure: Donald J. Black Resume

Perfect Reference Letter Example 4

In Example 4, the writer of the letter and the letter's target are managers in different divisions of the same company. Note how the writer subtly reminds the reader of a past favor.

Perfect Reference Letter Example 5

Example 5 is from a magnanimous employer whose employee is relocating. His letter to a man in a similar business in her new home town will get her interviewed—and most likely hired on the spot.

Perfect Reference Letter Example 6

The sixth example was written by an author and English professor to an executive at the publishing company that publishes his books. It should win the Pulitzer Prize for positioning. Study it and yours will, too!

Direct, concise, upbeat . . . brief, balanced, believable. All the reference letter examples presented in this chapter meet those criteria. All are written by properly positioned references, and they all position the applicant toward the target's office. Use them any way you like.

With such a singular introduction, the "director" who "screens" you will be expecting a superstar. Don't let your references—or yourself—down. Be prepared to follow up your perfect reference letters with a perfect interview. If you need help, read my contribution to your career casting, *The Complete Q&A Job Interview Book.*

Now, for the one person we avoided in almost all of the examples. Chapter 8 shows you how to get the perfect reference letter from your imperfect boss.

Example 4

——— American Foods Company ———
2204 Mercantile Building • Chicago • Illinois 60626
(312) 974-0700

Angela P. Edwards, Director
Market Research

April 3, 19__

Margaret O. Blaine, Product Manager
Convenience Foods Division
American Foods Company
1667 Commonwealth Avenue
Boston, Massachusetts 02210

Re: Amanda F. Harston Reference

Dear Marge:

I hope all is going well with your new product launch. Last
November, when my department gave you that revised market
research you needed, you asked me to let you know if you
could return the favor. Well, now you can.

My associate and friend, Amanda Harston, is applying for
the assistant product manager position that opened at the
breakfast division of American. In addition to great
credentials, Amanda has the energy, insight, and dedication
needed to be an outstanding assistant product manager.

As the enclosed resume shows, Amanda recently enhanced her
ten years' experience in product marketing at XYZ, Inc.,
with an MBA from Bentley College. She graduated with high
honors in spite of a 60-hour-a-week job that required 70
percent travel. Although she has moved up steadily at XYZ,
now that she has solid experience and graduate credentials,
she'd like a larger environment.

I know John Lawson, who is hiring for this position, will
interview Amanda if the request comes from you. It won't be
a waste of time. In fact, John will probably feel he owes
you a favor once he meets Amanda. Please pass her resume
along to him; she'll call John for an interview by the end
of the week.

Thanks in advance for your assistance.

Best regards,

Angela P. Edwards

APE:sae
Enclosure: Amanda Harston resume

Example 5

QUALITY MOTORS, LTD.
123 Elm Street
Appleton, Wisconsin 54911   •   (414) 868-1975

May 14, 19__

Anthony W. Michaels, President
Michaels Motors
10 Michigan Avenue
Milwaukee, Wisconsin 53208

Re: Lucille G. Anderson Reference

Dear Tony:

Although we haven't spoken in years (since that GM dealers
convention in Hawaii), I hope you'll carefully read this
letter.

I'm about to lose the best full-charge bookkeeper I've ever
known. Lucille Anderson has handled the books for all three
of my dealerships for the past 15 years, and is moving to
Milwaukee. Although I hate to see Lucy leave, I can't think
of a better businessman for her to see than you.

Lucy started working for us as a payroll clerk right after
she graduated from business college. She grew with the
business, and now manages a staff of seven bookkeepers and
clerks. She is personable, efficient, hardworking, and
almost never absent from work. Last year, when the IRS
audited us, everything checked completely. A number of
people have tried to hire Lucy away (including my own
C.P.A.), but she has remained loyal to us. I've taken the
liberty to enclose her resume. It should tell you all you
need to know.

Since you have a large dealership, I'm sure you can place
Lucille in a job that can use her capability. She'll call
you for an interview as soon as she gets settled at the end
of this month. If it works out, I wish you both the best.

Please call me after you've met. Thanks.

Very truly yours,

Charles L. Stanley

CLS:amr
Enclosure: Lucille G. Anderson Resume

Example 6

Colorado State University
Campus Parkway ▪ Denver ▪ Colorado 80110
(303) 579-5000

June 11, 19XX

Alicia E. Dunbar, Managing Editor
College Division
Oaktree Books Company
506 3rd Avenue
New York, New York 10158

Re: Melanie C. Berkman Reference

Dear Ms. Dunbar:

I am writing to recommend Melanie Berkman for the position
of editorial supervisor in your office.

My long association with Oaktree leads me to believe that
Melanie is the ideal employee for a company with such high
standards. She combines the ability to write with
organizational skills. She can grasp the requirements of a
program while effectively monitoring its details.

Melanie worked for me several years ago, before I accepted
a professorship. I wrote historical novels and directed the
Rocky Mountain Writers Center. She served as business
manager for the Center. Because Melanie took responsibility
for advertising, student enrollment, and tuition records, I
was able to concentrate on course development and teaching.
She also assisted me in the development of the manuscript
for one of my most important books.

A quick review of the enclosed resume should reveal that
Melanie's rare combination of experience and skill can
serve you well. She will call you within the next few days
to schedule an interview. When you meet her, I am sure you
will be convinced she is the right person for the job.

Thank you for your consideration.

Sincerely,

Benjamin T. Bellwood
Professor of English

BTB:lan
Enclosure: Melanie C. Berkman Resume

Chapter

8

Getting a Perfect Reference Letter from Your Present Supervisor

Chapter

8

Getting a Periodic
Reference Letter
from Your Present
Supervisor

This is usually not possible until your supervisor knows you are leaving. Most jobseekers don't mention they are looking for a job until they've found one. Therefore, the supervisor reference letter usually won't be a cover letter (discussed in Chapters 6 and 7) or a solicitation letter (coming up in Chapter 9). Although exceptions exist, most reference letters from a current supervisor are in the traditional "to-whom-it-may-concern" form.

If you are leaving your present job voluntarily, your present supervisor may not be a major factor in your current search. Most prospective employers exercise discretion in contacting present supervisors. Your direct supervisor is an important reference, though. His or her opinion will be sought and considered by all future prospective employers.

The time to get a reference letter from a supervisor is *before* your coworkers cut your cake. (I know—it's usually a cupcake or just the cup.) This letter will come in handy in the future if your supervisor runs away from home, goes crazy, dies, or tries to block your career path.

WHEN TO USE IT

Offer a neat, legible copy of this reference letter to interviewers when you believe the reference:

1. Can't be contacted by phone,

or

2. Shouldn't be.

The first reason is understandable, but be sure to explain it briefly. Don't get morbid about it or you'll raise suspicion that you're hiding the reference. It's like telling a child not to do something. (*Exactly* like it—most hiring could be appropriately conducted on a merry-go-round.)

But, if the security guards were called to break up a fight with your past supervisor, even a "courtesy" reference letter is no guarantee you're off the floor. Companies want to hear what direct supervisors have to say about you. You telegraph telephobia when your list of references omits them.

Case in Point

Consider the story of David Craven, who left the employ of Foster Manufacturing, Inc., under circus circumstances.

Foster was a small but successful closely held corporation when its two owners hired Craven to be the company's president.

All three had high hopes for the relationship. Craven had been an executive at a larger, public company in the same industry, and the two owners turned over management to him with expectations of soaring sales and improved operations.

Within a few months, it became painfully evident that Craven was not up to the job. After several attempts to improve matters, the owners decided the only solution was to fire him.

That was not the last of Craven, though. Within days, Foster was served with a lawsuit alleging wrongful termination. The settlement eventually included a reference letter, which read:

To Whom It May Concern:

This letter concerns David Craven, former President of Foster Manufacturing, Inc.

Mr. Craven's tenure with Foster was truly **remarkable**. While he held the position of President, from July 9, 19__ to September 29, 19__ the company's sales rose 45 percent over the same period the previous year. The company's asset base grew by 10 percent, and expenses as a percentage of revenue declined more than 20 percent.

Mr. Craven's most *significant* contributions included the implementation of new office procedures to streamline work. He also *extensively* studied several potential acquisitions.

We recommend Mr. Craven for any position that can employ his *particular* executive talents.

Sincerely,

XXXXXXXXXXXXXXX

Craven did not personally devise any of the measures that led to Foster's improvement. It was already growing, and the sales increases were part of a natural upswing.

But to honor the terms of their settlement and still maintain their own credibility, Foster's owners managed to draft a letter that was honest without being negative. They used adjectives ("remarkable," "significant," "particular") that were benign. This enabled them to present passive prose ("sales rose") that avoided giving Craven direct credit.

As for the "office management procedures," Craven had indeed been quite adept at interfering with the clerical staff and reorganizing their files—hardly the caliber of work the owners expected from their chief executive. But, they did give him credit for "streamlining" the office. He really did "extensively study" potential acquisitions, too—until they became extensively extinct.

As for his executive "talents," the owners were satisfied (if not ecstatic) with the words. They believed Craven should be working in a big company that needed an executive to mesmerize meetings and push papers. He just wasn't suited to their entrepreneurial approach which needed direct action.

They must have understood what I meant in *How to Turn an Interview into a Job*:

> One of the first things I learned in my personnel career was that people don't change, circumstances change. A typical example is the employee who is eased out of one company for poor work performance, then goes to another and becomes a superstar. Out of a bad marriage into a good one; failing at one school and becoming an honor student at another; the has-been actor who wins an Oscar. The opposite also occurs just as often.
>
> Sounds familiar, doesn't it? What is really happening?
>
> Nobody is changing, but different *circumstances* are bringing out different *attributes*. That is why internalizing failure is such an illogical, fallacious thing to do. (Internalizing success is illogical, too, but at least it gives you self-confidence.)
>
> Forget it—don't fight it. The face in the mirror will always be essentially the same. It's a lot easier to change your circumstances.[1]

MAKING A CIVIL REQUEST INSTEAD OF TAKING CIVIL ACTION

I don't recommend that you sue your employer just to compel a favorable reference. There's a big difference between being "terminated wrongfully" and *wrongful termination*. That difference can be very expensive. One day, Craven might present his "reference letter." The follow-up call might result in this response:

> **I'm sorry, I'm prevented by the terms of the settlement of a lawsuit from saying anything further. If you'd like more information than my letter provides, you can contact the following former employers . . .**

Reference referees shout "O-U-T out" at applicants who sued a former employer. And an agreement to forbear from disclosing litigation is unenforceable.

So be careful—you don't need a lawsuit to get a reference letter. In fact, most of the time you don't even need to threaten one.

MAKE THE BEST OF A BAD SITUATION

If you think you'll look like you're breakdancing in the dark when it comes to discussing your supervisor, reread Chapter 2. Remind him or her that the circumstances and chemistry were to blame. You might even quote my observation in *Surviving Corporate Downsizing*:

> Supervisor-subordinate relationships are undoubtedly among the oddest forms of human interaction. They are even stranger than kiwi birds at mating time. Ask any personnel professional.
>
> Hardly a day passed when some employee didn't wander into my office complaining about his boss. I'd ask, "Did you mention the problem to her?" You could write the script for the response: "No. You can't talk to her. She knows how I feel." The boss's version was quite different. She thought everything was fine. This scenario is played

thousands of times every day in human resources departments everywhere.

The reasons are extremely complex: Rivalry for power, latent parental resentment, lack of appreciation, unfairness, jealousy, favoritism, and an infinite number of others. You could try to figure them out until you're lowered down for the last time, so why bother? It's just nonproductive time and energy.[2]

If you had a tough time getting along with your supervisor, chances are that he or she had problems with you, too. Nobody gains from the strains and the pains. A reference letter can help your supervisor deal with the guilt over firing you. Think of yourself as a caregiver, not a victim.

Before you ask for a reference letter, review the positive aspects of your work at the company; then prepare a script like this between Ted (an employee), and Kathy (his supervisor).

Ted: I know we aren't parting company on the best of terms. But let's not allow a misunderstanding to erase all the success of the past few years.

I made many contributions to the department. I have positive reviews in my file and favorable memories of you, too. I respected your ability, even when I expressed disagreement with some of your views. We just had an honest difference of opinion. Don't you agree?

Kathy: I guess so. I'm sorry that it didn't work out, too. You have talent. I hated to fire you, but at some point I had to admit it wasn't a situation that could be changed.

Ted: I'm glad we agree on *that*, anyway. I've got a few good leads, and a recommendation from you would really help. Will you sign a letter that accentuates the positive?

Kathy: Sure, Ted. Why don't you draft something before the end of the day, and we'll discuss it.

In Ted's case, Kathy's letter can be targeted to specific individuals because he has already contacted prospective employers. In addition, he can draft one for her to sign for the future. The letter that Kathy, a no-nonsense kind of boss, agreed to sign is shown on the next page.

Kathy's letter is not a great reference, but a lot better than Ted's would have been. Instead of using his last moments at Marvel to seek revenge or speak his mind, he used the time wisely. It will pay dividends that could benefit him for the rest of his career.

No one likes to live with hostility. And when it comes to references, no one can. The longer you wait from the time you leave, the less you can influence the outcome.

You *can* survive involuntary termination and live with a forced reference. Once again, it's a matter of positioning. Cast the situation in the best possible light, then go on to the cast of another play. Besides, with all the positive reference resources you've got, an occasional sad supervisor sounds strange indeed.

I had one like that without knowing it. Every time I was hired, my new supervisor would tell me about how strange he was. Then one day I dropped a little law on him. He denied the bad rap. (They always do.) The next time he was called I was *really* embarrassed. I had to tell him to tone down his compliments. Not that they weren't *deserved*, mind you.

MARVEL PRODUCTS CORPORATION

667 Fair Street
Denver, Colorado 80112
(303) 234-6789

August 18, 19__

Bruce T. Hamrick, Plant Manager
Quality Manufacturing Company
25 Industrial Avenue
Shawnee, Kansas 66203

Re: Employment Reference for Theodore N. Ball

Dear Mr. Hamrick:

I am writing in reference to Ted Ball, who has applied for the position of Quality Assurance Supervisor with your company.

Mr. Ball held the position of Quality Assurance Supervisor at Marvel Products from 19__ to 19__. In that position, he reported to me. I found him to be exacting in his pursuit to eliminate any defects in Marvel's finished products. He upheld all quality control standards and was responsible for creating and implementing significant revisions to our procedures. These reduced rejects from 10 percent to under 5 percent.

Mr. Ball is a dedicated, uncompromising worker. He stands up for quality. I have great respect for his considerable talent.

If you have further questions of a specific nature, please contact me at (303) 234-6789.

Sincerely,

Kathleen R. Sullivan
Plant Manger

KRS:mew

Chapter

9

The Perfect Solicitation Letter from a Reference

A solicitation letter is also called a "broadcast letter." It broadcasts your talent and abilities to a wider audience through the power of a third-party testimonial. Unlike a specific letter, it is not personal to the target: Someone with the proper credentials just writes a letter about you aimed at appropriate senior executives.

Recruiters have used broadcast letters for years as a successful marketing technique for placing candidates. When a properly positioned colleague writes one, and you mass mail it directly, the results are even more effective.

PROFESSIONAL MARKETING KNOW-HOW

I have emphasized throughout that you are not just looking for a job, you are marketing your abilities to a specific consumer group—companies that need what you can do. When you know what professional marketeers know, you will be on top of the hireable heap on the decision maker's desk. You get noticed, called, interviewed, and offered a job.

DIRECT-MAIL DYNAMITE

This part of your marketing plan is a direct-mail campaign, with an important addition: telephone follow-up. Professional marketeers call this "phone/mail," and it has been proven to double—even triple—the results from direct mail alone.

You're running a campaign to improve your life—a campaign to get you more money, prestige, and career satisfaction. Follow the methods that the pros use, and you can't lose.

The proof of direct mail effectiveness fills your mailbox every day. The increase in the volume of direct mail over the past few years is astonishing. With the capacity of computer databases to locate, store, and retrieve information on everyone, based upon every possible profile and preference, focused direct mail is a multibillion-dollar-a-year industry.

Direct mail *works* because it is targeted. Unlike a commercial broadcast or advertising space, a direct-mail message does not compete with other advertisers for attention. If it gets to the interested party, and it gets opened, it gets from one to four minutes of the potential customer's undivided attention. This is more than any media advertising provides. That translates into more sales.

Direct mail is also the most scientific, controllable, and cost-effective method. A direct-mail, jobseeker marketing campaign outperforms any you-against-the-world, one-step-at-a-time approach to the job market. A phone/mail campaign leverages your time and gets your name in front of decision-makers faster. In your case, it's not only going to get your *name* in front of the decision-makers, but your *face* in front of them as well. From there, yours will be the new face on Placement Place.

The Reference

Select your very best reference—the one whose name or position will generate the most excitement. You can collaborate to create a reference cover letter suitable for top executives in all the companies you have targeted.

The Letter

The format you will use for this letter is identical to the Perfect Reference Letter Examples in Chapter 7. But, because the same letter is going to many "targets," you will have to omit personal "hooks."

This letter should not look mass-produced. Do not use "To Whom It May Concerns" photocopied onto copy paper. Each letter should be on high-quality (at least 24-pound) bond paper. The reference's letterhead, with raised type and watermark, is the best look for your letter.

If you have access to a word processor with a mail-merge program and a letter-quality printer, prepare originals on the reference's letterhead. A less effective way is to have an original typed neatly, and photocopy it on his or her letterhead. Then type in the name and address of each target. They should line up exactly as if they belonged there. Type the addresses on the same typewriter as the one used for the letter.

If the reference cannot supply you with 50 or more sheets of letterhead, you will have to resort to photocopies— but make sure they are on good, 24-pound *white* bond paper! It copies best, and the target may do a little internal mass mailing for you.

All letters should be signed individually by the reference. Envelopes should be typed individually; don't use a typed label.

This is personal correspondence, even if you do take some shortcuts to save time (and keep your reference happy). Think about your own reaction to mail solicitations. Which do you open first—the envelopes that look personalized or the ones that are obviously mass mailed?

Content of the Letter

The content should be just as sincere, measured, and factual as in all reference letters, but it must be *even more* riveting and convincing. You have only a few seconds to capture the readers' attention.

They'll look at the letterhead first. If that interests them, they'll glance down at the signature and read any "P.S." that appears below it. (Direct-mail pros pack their hardest sell into the P.S.). Finally, if they are still interested, they'll read the opening paragraph.

Each element of your letter must captivate your readers enough to go on. If they get to the opening paragraph, it has to be a real zinger to keep them reading. Study the example on the next page.

Use language and tone to sell value, to create interest, and to stimulate response. When you call, your target will be ready to talk.

THE LIST

Now, for your list of targets. Research your industry or profession exhaustively and get the names and contact information for key decision-makers in companies where you'd like to work. If you're not familiar with job search research, pick up copies of my paperbacks *How To Turn an Interview into a Job* and *The Complete Q&A Job Interview Book* for guidance.

In addition to the traditional sources of information on companies, some telephone sleuthing may turn up the information you need. One effective method is to call and identify yourself as a consultant working for a client. (You are— *you*.)

Say that your client provides services to that industry, and you would like the names of key personnel involved in acquiring your client's type of services. Know the names of the positions you are targeting: marketing directors, management information systems managers, production supervisors, and so

Sample Direct-Mail Letter

EMPLOYERS INSURANCE COMPANIES
Corporate Headquarters • One Founders Plaza
Hartford • Connecticut 06210 • (203) 526-0100

Henry V. Tattersall, III
Chief Financial Officer

January 15, 19__

Edgar O. Winston
Chief Financial Officer
General Investors Group
1200 Park Avenue
New York, New York 10011

Re: Joel M. Adams Reference

Dear Mr. Winston:

As Chief Financial Officers of multinational companies, you and I know how important the internal audit process is to our financial stability. But talented, skilled, effective audit managers are almost impossible to find.

My associate, Joel Adams, is one of them. A 20-year veteran of multinational audit management with direct responsibility to the CFO, Mr. Adams uses his keen understanding of the audit process to develop solutions to complex financial problems. His enclosed resume will illuminate his record at Wharton and his ability as an audit manager.

Mr. Adams reported directly to me in my former position as CFO at Amalgamated Industries. Amalgamated's acquisition by U.F.O. has placed him into the job market. I'm letting you know he is available in the event that you could benefit from the expertise of a highly qualified audit manager.

Please speak with Mr. Adams when he calls. I am confident it will be mutually beneficial.

Sincerely,

Henry V. Tattersall, III

P.S. Please let your secretary know that Joel Adams will be telephoning your office for an appointment within the week.

HVT:meg
Enclosure: Joel M. Adams resume

forth. Be businesslike and time-conscious. Sound like you know what you're doing. You do.

Direct mail is a numbers game. A well-written and produced, targeted direct-mail promotion can expect, at best, to get a 1.5 percent response. That's why mailings of one million pieces are commonplace.

No, you don't have to mail a million letters. But you should mail from 50 to 100. In a direct-mail campaign alone, you can expect only one or two targets to respond.

But, when conducting the far more effective phone-mail campaign, you call every one of your targets by the end of the week in which they receive your letter. From a mailing of 100 letters, you can expect at least 5, and maybe as many as 10, to arrange an interview. Otherwise, they'll give you the name of another individual who might be interested in your background.

WHEN TO MAIL

Timing the arrival of your letters is crucial. Monday morning usually brings more mail and messages. Fridays are for finishing and firing. Your letter should arrive on a Tuesday or Wednesday. By first-class mail, allow two to three days for delivery. Mail local letters on Monday, out-of-state letters on Friday.

WHEN TO CALL

You should call within two days of your letter's arrival. Once again, the Monday/Friday rule applies. If your letter arrived Tuesday or Wednesday, call on Thursday, between 9:00 A.M. and 10:00 A.M. (before the day's meetings start) or after 4:00 P.M. (when things have slowed down).

If you don't get through the first time, don't give up. If you do get through, talk to the target. Ask to meet with him personally. If he declines, don't hang up without getting the name of *another* decision-maker. Follow this script:

The Follow-Up Telephone Call Script

Version 1 (Target Is in His or Her Office and Interested):

Candidate: Hello, this is Joel Adams. My colleague, Mr. Tattersall, wrote to Mr. Winston about me. I'm calling to follow up on that letter. Is he available?

Secretary: One moment, I'll see if he can take your call, Mr. Adams. (Pause) Yes, Mr. Winston is available. I'll connect you now.

Target: Henry Winston.

Candidate: I'm Joel Adams, the audit manager our mutual friend Mr. Tattersall wrote about.

Target: Yes, Mr. Adams, I got the letter. Very impressive resume, too. I would like to talk to you some time next week. I'll give you back to my secretary and she can arrange it.

Candidate: Thank you. I look forward to meeting you.

Version 2 (Target Is in His or Her Office, No Position Available):

Candidate: Hello, this is Joel Adams. My colleague, Mr. Tattersall, wrote to Mr. Winston about me. I'm calling to follow up on that letter. Is he available?

Secretary: One moment, I'll see if he can take your call, Mr. Adams. (Pause) Yes, Mr. Winston is available. I'll connect you now.

Target: Henry Winston.

Candidate: I'm Joel Adams, the audit manager our mutual friend Mr. Tattersall wrote about.

Target: Hello, Mr. Adams. Yes, I received Henry's letter and your resume. I was very impressed with your credentials. However, I am sorry that I can't offer you any encouragement at the present time.

Candidate: I'm disappointed, too. I've long admired your operation. You have one of the finest reputations in the industry. Perhaps you know of someone else I could talk to?

Target: Yes, as a matter of fact, I do . . .

Version 3 (Target Is in a Meeting):

Candidate: Hello, this is Joel Adams. My colleague, Mr. Tattersall, wrote to Mr. Winston about me. I'm calling to follow up on that letter. Is he available?

Secretary: One moment, I'll see if he can take your call, Mr. Adams. (Pause) No, I'm sorry, sir, Mr. Winston is in a meeting and can't be disturbed.

Candidate: I understand, I'll be happy to call Mr. Winston at his convenience, if you'll tell me when he'll have a few minutes to talk.

Secretary: Hmm, let me see. He's scheduled for meetings all day, but he'll be in his office between 9 and 10 tomorrow.

Candidate: I'll call him at 9 tomorrow. Thank you.

Be sure to call back when you say you will. Your performance as a jobseeker signals the prospective employer what to expect of you as an employee.

Don't overload yourself. If you can't keep up with your follow-up phoning, your phone/mail campaign will fail. If you're sending 100 letters, don't schedule them all to arrive on the same Tuesday, because you'll never make 100 follow-up phone calls on Thursday of the same week. You don't want your name to have faded from their memory when you do call.

Generally, you can make about 25 follow-up phone calls a day and still sound enthusiastic each time. Therefore, your phone/mail campaign will take about a month to complete. In the meantime, you'll be going on interviews and feeling confident as your jobgetting skills improve.

Be realistic. If you're still working and you *know* you'll never get time away from your job to make 25 personal calls, reduce the number of letters you send each week and extend your campaign over a longer period of time.

Sending and calling on 50 to 100 letters should net you five to ten interviews. Using *The Complete Q&A Job Interview Book*, the average applicant gets one offer for every three interviews, so you should have at least three offers by the end of your campaign. But there's more to know about references. It's coming up in the next three chapters.

Chapter

10

The Perfect Inclusion Letter

In Chapter 2, I said you had to discipline yourself and fit your entire job history into a *one-page*, focused resume. The nature of the job market today demands that you adhere to this rule. Write more and you have even less chance of being read. Write in generalities and you won't hit the target directly.

An inclusion letter is a cover letter for a resume that expands and customizes it. The letter can explain an employment gap or illuminate an area of your experience to turn that printed page into an 8 1/2-by-11-inch portrait.

Follow the form recommended for reference cover letters. Make your inclusion letter brief (again, no more than one page), interesting, and professional. *Personalize* it.

In developing the content, review the specific job or company you have targeted. Study your targets to learn what is most important to them, and what you have that they need. Then drive your point home with a few riveting paragraphs that will get you an interview.

VARIATIONS ON THE THEME

An inclusion letter can be sent by itself. This is appropriate in response to a reference letter reply. The first paragraph of the letter acknowledges the response. Then the resume is expanded and customized further.

An inclusion letter also can be formatted as a follow-up letter after the interview. You might want to mention an article you wrote or amplify some area of your expertise. Since it is timed *after* you know the spectators' specifications, you can play to the stands.

It's helpful to use something discussed during the interview as a "hook" to start you selling. Following are examples of inclusion letters. Copy whatever you like. Then you can write me.

The items you must communicate for the target job should be done with the inclusion letter. Be honest, not modest.

Use your perfect inclusion letter to show how your unique combination of character, skill, and experience makes *you* the perfect candidate for the job.

Perfect Inclusion Letter Example 1

124 Atwater Avenue
Darby, Pennsylvania 19023

September 24, 19__

Gloria S. Cooper
Director of Operations
Bakery Division
International Food Corporation
100 Corporate Park
Wilmington, Delaware 19899

Re: Construction Manager Position

Dear Ms. Cooper:

I am writing in response to your September 21, 19__ ,
advertisement in <u>The Wall Street Journal</u> for a Construction
Manager to oversee your retail operations.

As the enclosed resume reveals, I have 20 years experience
in the development and operation of commercial real estate.
It ranges from site selection to completed properties. The
resume does not mention that I brought every one of 50
multimillion-dollar construction projects in under budget
and ahead of schedule.

Successful operations depend on a knowledgeable, attentive
construction manager. If you don't select the right site,
plans, and contractor, and complete construction within
budget and time parameters, the project may never succeed.
Therefore I have developed a systematic approach to ensure
attention to details by a competent crew.

I am particularly experienced in the regions of the country
targeted by your advertisement, having been the
Construction Manager for the Hughes retail clothing chain
from 1980 to 1985. The mid-Atlantic states have unique
labor and distribution problems, and I know the solutions
to them.

You will see from reviewing my resume that I possess the
qualifications and skills you seek, and I look forward to
the opportunity to meet you in person and discuss the
position.

Sincerely,

Andrew J. Barton, Jr.

Perfect Inclusion Letter Example 2

25 Church Street
Mystic, Connecticut 06355

October 7, 19__

Thomas R. Gould
Creative Director
White Advertising Company
222 Madison Avenue, Suite 1000
New York, New York 10017

Dear Mr. Gould:

Your advertisement in *Advertising Age* for a graphic
designer for fashion layouts caught my attention. The
position is precisely the kind of opportunity I seek. My
resume is enclosed. As you can see, my experience matches
your specifications.

You'll note I have more than 10 years design experience for
three different agencies. In all three positions, I worked
extensively on fashion layouts. I also worked for three
years as the lead graphic designer for Bloomingdale's in-
house agency. My portfolio includes display advertising,
and catalog and point-of-purchase design.

While I have been away from the employment scene for five
years raising my daughter, I have supervised several
freelance projects. Most recently, I designed the show
catalog for the St. Laurent fall fashion line. Now that my
daughter is in school, I am ready to return to agency
graphic design full time and can't think of a better place
to contribute than White Advertising.

I welcome the opportunity to meet you and show you my
complete portfolio. I'll call you within the week to
schedule an interview.

Sincerely,

Melanie D. Foster

Perfect Inclusion Letter Example 3

125 North Water Street
Boston, Massachusetts 02117

November 3, 19__

Robert L. Woodman
Administrator
Sloane Memorial Medical Center
135 Memorial Drive
Harrisburg, Pennsylvania 17105

Re: Assistant Administrator Position

Dear Mr. Woodman:

Donald Sievers, Administrator of Humanity Hospital in San
Antonio, Texas, wrote you recently regarding my
qualifications for the position of Assistant Administrator
at your hospital. Mr. Sievers enclosed my resume for your
review.

I am writing in anticipation of a question or two you might
have concerning my resume. Although my career in health
care management has progressed in responsibility and range,
my resume shows no employment from September, 1981 through
May, 1983. I took those 21 months to work full time on my
Masters in Health Care Management at Temple University. It
wouldn't have been possible to do justice to my studies
while working my typical 60-hour week as Reimbursement
Program Administrator at Children's Hospital in
Philadelphia.

I earned my Master's Degree with Distinction, and was
immediately recruited by Humanity Hospitals, Inc., as Chief
Auditor for the Northeast, beginning June 1983. Two
promotions later, I am now in charge of Humanity's audit
staff. That position has afforded me a rare opportunity to
become intimately acquainted with the operations of dozens
of hospitals nationwide. I know what works and what
doesn't, and I believe I can be an asset to Sloane Memorial
as Assistant Administrator.

I will call you by week's end to see if you'd like to
schedule a meeting to discuss how my skills and experience
can benefit Sloane Memorial.

Sincerely,

Walter D. Chessman

Perfect Inclusion Letter Example 4

15587 Russell Street
Greenville, South Carolina 29602

December 5, 19__

Abigail N. Hardesty
Director of Human Resources
Quality Furniture Manufacturers, Inc.
1500 Magnolia Boulevard
Charleston, South Carolina 29401

Re: Third Shift Production Manager Position

Dear Ms. Hardesty:

Your advertisement in the most recent edition of the <u>Sunday Star Ledger</u> called for a seasoned production manager to handle third-shift operations at your Durham, North Carolina, plant.

The enclosed resume reflects that I am well qualified for the position, with over 25 years furniture manufacturing experience. After graduation from high school, I began as an equipment operator and progressed through scheduling, purchasing, and inventory control to my current position as Production Manager of the first shift at Rosewood Furniture's Greenville plant. The challenge of managing Quality's much larger operation in Durham ignited my interest.

The "minimum educational requirements" specified in your ad were a Bachelor's Degree in business administration, manufacturing management, <u>or its equivalent</u>. When I began my career in 1964, a college education was not a prerequisite for rising through the manufacturing ranks. Through extension study and "on-the-job training," I have gained experience in all facets of the production environment. In fact, it is probably equivalent to several college degrees.

Rotating shift schedules have hampered my ability to attend all of the night classes for a degree, but I have managed to accumulate 65 credits toward a Bachelor of Science in Administration with a concentration in Manufacturing Management, and I intend to keep working until I've completed it.

I'll telephone you within the next week to set a convenient meeting date.

Very truly yours,

Thomas Y. Crowell

Perfect Inclusion Letter Example 5

16 Fox Hill Road
Fairfield, Connecticut 06430

January 19, 19__

Sylvester T. Coe
Vice President of Operations
Trumbull Manufacturing
514 Bridgeport Avenue
Trumbull, Connecticut 06611

Re: Energy Manager Position

Dear Mr. Coe:

I enjoyed our meeting yesterday and our discussions regarding your requirements for an Energy Manager to supervise your foundry operations. I mentioned that I would get you copies of several articles I've written about conservation and load management for energy trade publications.

I'm sending you copies of three articles that apply to the kind of manufacturing operation you have. You can see from their content that I've spent a great deal of time in the foundry environment and have been successful in reducing energy costs. I've achieved results of 15 to 45 percent reduction in peak usage, which has translated to hundreds of thousands of dollars in energy savings each year for clients.

As Trumbull's full-time Energy Manager, I estimate I can save you at least five times my salary in the first year. My experience has given me great insight that I'm eager to put into practice at Trumbull Manufacturing.

If you have any questions pertaining to the articles, please don't hestitate to call. I hope to hear from you soon.

Very truly yours,

Michael C. Malone

Chapter

11

Formats for Perfect Follow-Up Letters

A follow-up letter can—and should—be much more than an oversized thank-you note. Fortunately for you, 95 percent of them are nothing more. If they're sent at all, they have no effect. Lackluster and unimaginative, these overworked form letters can even stop germinating a job offer. They apologize, de-emphasize, and jeopardize your chances.

FOLLOW-UP TO A PHOTO FINISH

The placement race is like any other: To win, you must maintain or increase your pace. You've trained and conditioned yourself, prepared for the job of your life every step of the way—through resumes, references, and interviews. You've done fine so far, but if you fail to communicate properly after the interview, you might just as well have rested. Someone else will cross the finish line. There's only one winner.

A follow-up letter gives you the boost you need. It works so well because the interviewer is confused. There are simply too many resumes, too many candidates, and too many people in the hiring cycle to satisfy. That's why recruiters are trained to limit the number of referrals. More than three "send outs" for any opening is considered counterproductive. The probability of placing someone is a statistical zero.

That's why a follow-up letter is so effective. It "unconfuses" the interviewer by giving him or her a reason to make a decision. It restates the areas you want to emphasize, and can even change your profile completely. Inconsistencies disappear because the new data automatically erases the old. It's like typing over something on a computer screen. The interviewer's brain can't comprehend the inconsistency, so the new data etches over the old. You can actually "re-interview" over original mistakes, and underline, highlight, and otherwise rewrite your qualifications.

Of course, this doesn't work if the interviewer is still cleaning up his or her office from your disaster. But then again, he or she would be too busy to read your letter anyway.

I dealt with this subject in *How to Turn an Interview into a Job*:

> All those words you said during the interview have dwindled down to one or two remarks, and your image is fading fast. The danger is that you will be grouped with other applicants. Now is the time to rekindle some of those fond old memories and restate your image.[1]

By now, you should be well on your way to writing letters that are read. Let's use some techniques to follow up on them.

FOLLOW-UP LETTER TECHNIQUE

Style and Substance

Limit your letter to one page with three to five well-written, enthusiastic, informative paragraphs. Use only quality stationery, and proofread each letter carefully. Have your follow-up letters in the mail the business day after your interview.

To the novice, jobgetting appears to be a high-stakes gamble. But it's really one of the most predictable (and, therefore, controllable) areas of human interaction. Fortunately for you, it's misunderstood by almost everyone else running in the placement race.

The perfect follow-up letter, like the perfect reference letter, combines the *science* of specific formats with the *art* of communication. You should reiterate your primary assets and accomplishments, and convincingly describe how you can benefit the employer. The properly spelled names of people you met and buzzwords familiar to the interviewer should be included carefully, and your letter should request a reply as soon as possible.

1. Address Line

Include the full company name, full address (no abbreviations), full name of the interviewer, and his or her full title. These make you look fully professional.

2. Subject Line

"Re: Interview for the Position of Operations Manager on June 11, 19XX"

This gets attention and focuses on the contents of the letter.

3. Greeting

"Dear Mr. (Ms.) Lathrop:"

"Miss" or "Mrs." should not be used unless you know the interviewer does so. First names are not appropriate even if they were used during the interview.

4. Opening

a. "It was a pleasure meeting with you last Tuesday to discuss the opening in the Operations Department with The Tramell Company."

b. "I appreciated meeting with Jill Anderson and yourself in your office on Thursday to discuss the Marketing Analyst position with Indiana Power and Light Company.

c. "Thanks again for your courtesy in taking the time to see me regarding the opening in Systems Communications."

5. Body

Develop something discussed during your interview in the body of the letter. Choose a topic that allows you to emphasize how your qualifications will help the employer. This will turn your follow-up into far more than a thank-you note.

a. "From our discussion, and the fine reputation of your organization, it appears that the branch manager position would enable me to fully utilize my background in financial management."

b. "I was particularly impressed with the professionalism of those I met. Quality Products Corporation appears to have the kind of environment I have been seeking."

c. "The atmosphere at H. Price Company seems to strongly favor individual involvement, and I would undoubtedly be able to contribute significantly to its goals."

6. Closing

a. "While I have been considering other situations, I have deferred a decision until hearing from you. Therefore, your prompt reply would be appreciated."

b. "It's an exciting opportunity, and I'm looking forward to hearing your decision soon."

c. "The cost accountant position and Multiflex Manufacturing Company are exactly what I have been seeking, and I hope to hear from you within the next week."

7. Salutation

"Sincerely,"
"Very truly yours,"
"Best regards,"

Now let's take a look at a few interviews and the follow-up letters that turned them into jobs.

Perfect Follow-Up Letter Example 1

The writer of this letter interviewed for the position of sales representative with a leading pharmaceutical manufacturer. During her interview, the sales manager suggested she lacked enough experience.

Perfect Follow-Up Letter Example 2

This letter was written to the head of a search committee looking for a principal of a junior high school. The applicant must position himself as the one perfect choice among hundreds.

Perfect Follow-Up Letter Example 3

The final example clinched the job of department manager for a man who had never held that title.

Note how all three examples hardly even resemble thank-you letters. They're personalized, fast-moving, and concise. In each letter, the applicant has "connected" with the recipient. The words are read and responded to.

Example 1

2625 Greenfield Avenue
El Paso, Texas 79910

May 14, 19__

Steven R. Cummings
National Sales Manager
Prizm Pharmaceuticals Corporation
1050 Industrial Parkway
Jacksonville, Florida 32201

Re: Interview for the Position of Sales Representative,
    Southwest Territory, on May 9, 19__.

Dear Mr. Cummings:

Thank you for your courtesy during our meeting on Tuesday.
The continued success of Prizm Pharmaceuticals offers just
the kind of career challenge I have been seeking.

In my former positions as both a product detailer and a
sales representative for a hospital products company, I
dealt extensively with the two types of clients I will
encounter in the Prizm position: physicians and hospital
purchasing agents.

Further, my undergraduate degree in biology combined with
Prizm's training program will give me the background I need
to knowledgeably discuss its products and their
effectiveness. I am a "quick study," as my college and work
record has shown.

I am able to travel and devote the time necessary to build
this new territory for Prizm. As a lifelong resident of the
Southwest, I am familiar with the territory and
characteristics of the people.

I have what it takes to be a top member of your team, and
I'd like to work with you to achieve your sales objectives.

I look forward to hearing from you next week.

                              Best regards,

                              Lindsey N. Crawford

Example 2

1250 Plains Road
Joliet, Illinois 60459

April 20, 19___

Doris C. Birnbaum, Chair
Search Committee
Elm City Board of Education
2040 Lincoln Avenue
Elm City, Illinois 61529

Re: Interview for principal vacancy, April 19, 19___.

Dear Ms. Birnbaum:

It was a pleasure to meet with you and the rest of the
committee last night. I particularly appreciated the time
to discuss my qualifications as principal of Steiger Junior
High School.

As a member of the Joliet Board of Education, I helped
select the vice-principal for our high school last year.
You've no doubt narrowed the field down to several
qualified candidates, but there's always the question: "How
do you know he or she will have the right combination of
firm authority, helpfulness, and caring persuasiveness?"

Of course, you never know until someone actually occupies
the position. As both an educator and a parent of junior
high students, I don't just understand your concerns, I
live them. Of paramount importance to a junior high school
principal should be the task of assisting students through
this developmental period with their education and self-
esteem enhanced. I believe that success comes from
listening to students and teachers, and from being a good
manager.

This position is a critical one that affects the lives of
thousands of young people in your district. Your citizens
are fortunate that the decision rests with a dedicated
search committee.

I look forward to hearing from you soon.

Sincerely,

Thomas R. O'Connor

Example 3

---

66 Parker Avenue
Bergenfeld, New Jersey 07201

July 10, 19__

Harvey D. Anderson
Director of Marketing
Fuels Division
American ChemCo, Inc.
1250 River Road
Newark, New Jersey 07601

Re: Interview for Manager of Marketing Planning, July 6, 19__.

Dear Mr. Anderson:

Thank you for the time and attention you gave me in my interview on Thursday.

I agree that today's "manager" is a team leader who must educate and motivate his staff, then allow them to use their initiative toward achieving the desired results. Today's organizational members are highly educated, motivated, and intelligent. They perform best when "managed" indirectly.

Although my title has never been "manager," my work record demonstrates that that has been my function. In achieving results, I have influenced people at all levels across the organization. That experience qualifies me to lead and motivate the six people who will report to the Manager of Marketing Planning.

My graduate studies in management taught me the theory of management. My experience taught me the practical aspects of selecting and motivating people. This, combined with my own record as an exemplary employee, demonstrates the kind of manager I will be.

I'd like to start my career in management as the Manager of Marketing Planning in your division. I hope you'll be calling soon.

Very truly yours,

Eric T. Winslow

Chapter

12

The Perfect Follow-Up Telephone Call

The follow-up telephone call is one of the most important devices in the job search and also one of the most unused. Knowing *whom* to call, *when* to call, and *how* to call can restate your image at the most crucial stage of the hiring process: the post-interview evaluation.

Call the wrong person, and you might just as well be calling yourself. Call too early or too late, and you've wasted your "one phone call." Call improperly, and you'll hear some version of "Don't call us, we'll call you." But call the way I suggest and you can get the best job of your career.

Fear of rejection keeps most applicants away from the phone. They internalize negative responses until "rejection shock" occurs. Heart palpitations when talking with prospective employers is the major symptom, if its victims ever get that far. The proper approach to phone follow-up is the cure. Use it and you'll contract *acceptance* shock!

In his best-selling book *Power! How to Get It, How to Use It*, Michael Korda stated, "The person who receives a telephone call is always in an inferior position of power to the person who placed it."[1] When combined with your general anxiety about being hired, this can push your foot out of the interviewer's door while waiting for a call. It's up to you: Will it be, "Don't call us, we'll call you," or, "Please call us, we're too (busy, disorganized, confused, etc.) to call you."?

That's exactly what I did to get the best job of my career. I took a deep breath and called the vice president and general counsel of a major bank. He was in charge of hiring for the position I wanted. This is how it went:

JGA: (Deep breath) Hello, Mr. _____. This is Jeff Allen. I'm calling to thank you for interviewing me for the legal assistant position.

AMR: (In a hurried, distracted tone) Right. I have your resume on the pile in front of me. I'm glad you called! That's one less decision I have to make. You've got the job. Start the first of the month.

Talk about acceptance shock! It was all I could do to keep from running over to my boss and giving notice. I called the personnel office at least a dozen times with creative questions just to be sure I hadn't been dreaming (an occupational hazard for night law students with day jobs).

When *you* make the phone call, sounding confident and assured, you really *are* in control. You have the facts about the best possible candidate—you—immediately available. You have a second, critical chance to emphasize your professionalism, confidence, and job skills. AMR didn't stand a chance; on my start date he confessed he couldn't even remember who I *was*!

If your timing is right, your target will be reviewing resumes when you call. You're the only candidate with a persuasive, intelligent spokesperson on the line at that moment, and you, therefore, improve your chances dramatically.

KNOWING THE RIGHT PLACE AND TIME

How many times have you seen someone get hired and thought, "Hmmm. He's no smarter than I am. He was just in the right place at the right time."

It's true. But do you tell yourself that as an excuse or an explanation? Aren't you just thinking, "He was lucky"? As long as you think that way, you'll never see his secret of success.

He knew where and when to get hired. You're learning how.

Now you must *create* that opportunity to go the distance. Sit comfortably at your desk, back straight, confident. Take a deep breath, exhale slowly, and make the call that will get you hired.

WHOM TO CALL

In almost every case, you will call the person who interviewed you and received your follow-up letter. When several people are involved, determine the most influential, and call him or her.

WHEN TO CALL

Don't Wait Too Long

The best approach to take is the "fiddle theory." It was introduced by Robert Ringer in *Winning Through Intimidation*:

> The longer a person fiddles around with something, the greater the odds that the result will be negative. . . . In the case of Nero, Rome burned; in the case of a sale, the longer it takes to get to a point of closing, the greater the odds it will never close.
>
> As a general rule, you should assume that time is always against you when you try to make a deal—any kind of deal. There's an old saying about "striking while the iron's hot," and my experience has taught me that it certainly is a profound statement in that circumstances always seem to have a way of changing.[2]

Concentrate on a well-drafted letter like the examples shown in Chapter 11, keep the pressure on the employer, and don't let up on your interview scheduling. If you haven't received a response to your follow-up letter *within a week* after the interview, call.

Never on a Monday

Mondays are full of staff meetings, unexpected crises, and weekend wounds. Don't call, write, or interview on a Monday if you can help it. Statistically, the best time to call is Tuesday through Friday, from 9:00 A.M. to 11:00 A.M.

WHAT TO SAY

Although I have emphasized that you are selling your skills and abilities to the highest bidder, one rule of the sale does *not* apply here. Don't "ask for the job."

It always surprises sales professionals when I give this advice, but I do it because I want to save you from looking like you're on your hands and knees. That's the wrong position to be in to interview properly.

The correct position is sitting erect and considering several offers. Instead of asking for the job, your pressure point is an *answer*, because you have "waited as long as you can," have "some decisions to make," and so on. Your firm but gentle tone will convey that message even though your words don't.

GETTING THROUGH

This time, you're not just a name, so it will be easier to get through the gatekeeper to the individual you want. If you have trouble, treat the executive's secretary or assistant as your ally, not your adversary. A courteous, firm tone of voice works wonders. Don't play games to get around the front desk: Businesspeople use their names and state the purpose of their calls. Don't ask annoying questions about the boss's schedule, hoping to catch him or her unguarded. A good gatekeeper won't tell you. In any case, if you call very early (before 9:00 A.M.) or late (after 5:00 P.M.) you can often hit your target directly.

If You Speak to the Secretary

Secretary: Good morning, Mr. Wagner's office.

You: This is Donna Boardman calling. May I speak to him, please?

Secretary: I'm sorry, he's away from his desk/on another line/ in a meeting. May I take a message?

You: Mr. Wagner and I met last week regarding the engineering manager position.

Secretary: One minute please.

The boss might very well be away from his desk, on another line, or in a meeting. But probably the secretary is checking to see whether he wants to take the call. If not:

You: When would be a good time to call him back? (or) I'll hold on, if it won't tie up your line.

Since you have been direct and cooperative, the secretary is inclined to return the courtesy. Also be polite and stubborn: you'll get through before long.

And when you do, here's the script:

Interviewer: Ed Wagner.

You: Hello, Mr. Wagner. (Note: Use "Miss" or "Mrs." only if you know the interviewer does so.)

This is Donna Boardman.

Interviewer: Hello. I got your follow-up letter just a couple days ago. No decision has been made yet, but I assure you that you're still being considered for the position.

You: That's good news. As I said in my letter, I'm very interested. I know I would be a good fit for the job. However, I'm in a difficult situation. I've been asked for a decision on another offer and I've delayed as long as I can. I'd really rather work for Allied Equipment. Can you tell me when exactly I should hear from you?

Interviewer: I understand. Let me see what I can do. I can tell you you're one of two remaining candidates. I have a meeting with the director at 3:00 to go over this. I'll push for a decision.

You: Great! I really appreciate it. Shall I call you at 4:00?

Interviewer: Better make it 4:30.

You: I'll talk to you then. Thank you.

Interviewer: Goodbye.

You: Goodbye.

Now *that's* a follow-up phone call charged with positive energy. It's almost certain that you will be the decision the decision-maker makes.

Even if you and the other candidates are *equally* qualified, you're the one who will be calling back for the news, and most hiring officials avoid giving bad news more than jobseekers avoid receiving it. You've given yourself a formidable edge. And your competitors won't even know why they lost the race.

While you're always at an advantage if you catch the decision-maker in the midst of pondering his or her decision, you're still ahead even if you catch him or her off guard. As I mentioned earlier, that's the way I got hired for that legal assistant job.

Here's how your "close encounter of the hiring kind" might go:

Decision-Maker: Oh, yes, Ms. Boardman. Let me see if I remember correctly. You were the engineer with an MBA from, where was it, San Francisco State University?

You: No, that must have been *another* candidate. *My* MBA is from Stanford. I graduated with high honors two years ago from their Executive Management Program. I have 15 years experience as a senior engineer for Standard Products Company.

Decision-Maker: Now I remember. Very impressive credentials.

You: (Your best line) I have the combination of education and experience to do the job you need done. I'd be surprised if you've run across *anyone* better prepared than I am.

Decision-Maker: No, that's true. But we have other things to consider.

You: Are you at liberty to discuss them?

Decision-Maker: Well, for example, we're concerned about bringing in someone from the outside. The department resulted from the merger of two others. There have been staff layoffs, and the job requires someone who can improve morale. An outsider may not be able to do that.

You: If you review my reference letters, you'll note that the people who have worked for me have spoken highly of my skills as a team builder. Maybe an outsider is just what you need for this touchy situation. Someone without a history at the company, with no preconceived ideas and hidden agendas. I think I'm that person.

Decision-Maker: That's an excellent point, and it probably just won you the game, Ms. Boardman. When did you say you can start?

You: With two weeks notice to my current employer, I can be there.

Decision-Maker: I'll send the papers to personnel today.

You: Thank you, Mr. Wagner. I look forward to working with you. I know you'll be convinced you selected the right person for the job.

Follow these guidelines step by step, and you'll be where you want to be, doing what you want to do.

Hundreds of the "closers" professional recruiters use are contained in *Closing on Objections* by Paul Hawkinson. The book isn't available to jobseekers, but since Paul is my placement partner, write "Jeff sent me" on your letter when ordering it. That and your check will have you roaming around companies you never dreamed would let you in. Ordering information is contained in the Bibliography.

Now let's discuss the two remaining obstacles that trip unsuspecting jobseekers—government records and gaps in employment history.

Chapter

13

The Legal Aspects of References

Even a decade ago, few lawsuits were brought by employees alleging wrongful termination, discrimination, or damaged reputation. But the last ten years have seen a surge in the number of workers dragging their employers into court. As an article in the July 1989 issue of *Nation's Business* pointed out:

> Costly legal combat pitting employees and former employees against employers is expanding rapidly as workers in unprecedented numbers look to the courts to resolve all manner of workplace controversies—from job security to parental leave. And many of those plaintiffs are walking away with judgments reaching into the millions. . . .
>
> Jury Verdict Research, Inc., a private organization that monitors jury decisions throughout the country in cases involving claims of physical, emotional, and mental injury, reports that a former employee claiming wrongful discharge has an 86 percent chance of winning a case brought against a private business or industry, as opposed to a 33 percent probability for a suit against a government entity.[1]

Threat of costly litigation—and multimillion-dollar awards—has caused most companies to institute policies that restrict what employees can say in response to reference checks. Most instruct employees to do nothing more than confirm dates of employment. Therefore, nothing really useful to a hiring company can be said. Some companies prohibit responding to reference-check calls at all!

There are even *statutes* in many states making it *illegal* for employers to give any information about an employee who has been fired. Usually only dates of employment can be released. In this environment, the prospective employer risks a lawsuit for *negligent hiring* by not checking thoroughly. Bradford Smart noted in *The Smart Interviewer*:

> Actually, the situation is worse than described. Courts are increasingly finding companies like yours *liable* for hiring bad guys (rapists, for example) because your company failed to perform record checks! . . . How's that for a catch 22? It's prudent for companies to withhold information on former employees, but companies are vulnerable to litigation if they don't check prospective employees' records.[2]

The person responsible for making a hiring decision is hopelessly helpless. Hiring the wrong person is costly, but getting objective information to make a decision is practically impossible. The difficult and delicate process of getting any information at all makes an applicant who volunteers references more valuable than ever. At least the hiring authority can say he or she relied on *something*!

GOOD REFERENCES ARE AN EDGE

The litigious atmosphere surrounding hiring and firing today makes it more important than ever to develop good references and use them in your job search. The applicant who "waives" his or her right to prevent disclosure, then *facilitates* it, is a supersearcher indeed.

In spite of policies prohibiting the giving of references, hiring officials still attempt to check references in order to learn more about a candidate before hiring him or her. And for good reason, claimed Smart:

> Interviewing should not be deadly serious, but the selection process *is*. In 20 years I have witnessed more mismatch carnage than I care to think about. Square pegs in round holes have resulted in suicides, drug problems, company failures, foolish-appearing hiring managers, and a lower GNP.
>
> The typically silly match-making dance in which interviewers ask the wrong questions about a partial list of person specifications and interviewees come prepared to hype strengths and hide shortcomings is ludicrously shallow, superficial, and harmful—to hiring managers and candidates alike. . . .
>
> You, the hiring manager, have every legal right and moral *obligation* to thoroughly investigate the strengths and weaker points of a candidate in relation to all the person specifications. You can look a candidate in the eye and say with pride:
>
> *You cannot afford to make a wrong job choice and neither can I, so let's be as thorough as we both can be in the hiring process.*[3]

The right job is far more important to an applicant than it is to an employer. To an employer it's only money; to an applicant it's a livelihood—a life. This chapter is designed to help the person reduce its impact. However, anyone dependent on another for his or her livelihood should know his or her rights and liabilities.

Let's review the laws and general guidelines most employers observe to help you understand the employer's perspective. Then you can use it to your advantage. Here's some of the advice I gave employers in *The Employee Termination Handbook*:

Almost universally, there are conflicting needs after terminating an employee: A need to rationalize internally, and a need to reconcile externally. This creates a tendency to explain the termination internally in the harshest possible light—certainly there was abundant cause. But externally, the normal reaction is to minimize the fault, do a good turn for the employee you are now rid of—give him or her an exaggerated recommendation. Both reactions, though instinctive, are wrong in terms of potential litigation.

The harsh statements internally may create a valid defamation claim, or at the least an active sympathy on a jury. Either result can be very costly. To compound the problem, when you give a good report externally, you buttress the plaintiff's case that the termination was improper. Yet you get a bad report, you defame your former employee. The only proper answer is employment dates, jobs performed, and with authorization, ending wage or salary. When you go beyond those bare-bones facts, you increase the risk of an action for bad-mouthing or for wrongful termination bolstered by the esteem and value placed on the employee's services in the reference check.

The high road and the low road being risky, take the middle and give only objective data about which there can be no argument. In this context "name, rank, and serial number" translates into dates of employment (starting and ending dates), classifications held and, if authorized, wage/salary earned at the time of separation. Nothing more; do not comment on the employee's reason for leaving; work record in a qualitative sense, that is beyond classifications held; or his or her eligibility for rehire. Name, rank and serial number only. And tell your supervisors to say the same thing or, better yet, refer all calls regarding former employers to human resources or personnel.[4]

That means one of two things to a candidate. One who was

terminated is probably protected by law from negative references. But one with an exemplary work record has an incredible advantage.

Every high performer has to *prove* his or her worth, and the best way is with references. You may need to give written authorization to past supervisors to reveal subjective information about your past. If the interviewer doesn't ask for such written authorization, you can volunteer it.

If you were fired, here's more advice to employers you should know about from *The Employee Termination Handbook*:

> Because terminated employees have an obligation to minimize any damages resulting from termination (the obligation to "mitigate" damages), the employer has an obvious interest in the placement of former employees, both from a moral and a pecuniary viewpoint.[5]

As this notes, an employer who fired you has a strong interest in making sure you find another job—fast. It's probably not necessary to sue for a reference, or even to *threaten* legal action to get one.

Remember what I wrote in Chapter 8: "Different *circumstances* bring out different *attributes*." You can survive a poor reference without finding someone else to blame. After all, learning from past mistakes is the most effective form of education there is. Using this justification, you are in an excellent position to negotiate a helpful, if not complimentary, reference from that company.

ENSURING THE RIGHT THINGS ARE SAID ABOUT YOU

Now for a look at the laws that give you a course of action if an employer deliberately makes false, demeaning statements about you. Many state legislatures have enacted *antiblacklisting* and *service letter statutes* that go far beyond common law by mandating that employers give only truthful oral and written job references when an employee leaves.

Antiblacklisting Statutes

Antiblacklisting statutes punish employers for maliciously or even knowingly attempting to prevent former employees from finding work. Service letter statutes require them to furnish employees with written statements of the cause for dismissal or the reasons for their resignation. The employer can't use reasons other than those in the service letter. Arkansas, California, Connecticut, Florida, Indiana, Iowa, Kansas, Maine, Missouri, Montana, Nebraska, New Hampshire, New Mexico, North Carolina, Ohio, Oklahoma, Texas, Utah, Virginia, and Washington are among the states that have laws of this type.

Service Letter Statutes

Service letter statutes require employers to give truthful reference letters if former employees request them. Some states with laws like this are Florida, Indiana, Idaho, Kansas, Maine, Missouri, Montana, and Nebraska. The majority of these statutes require no more than a statement of the reason the employee left. Missouri and Kansas require that the employer state the nature of the service (job) as well. Kansas mandates that employers state length of employment, job classification, and wage rate. Some laws punish *truthful* statements of the reasons for an employee's departure, too. It's not a bad idea, considering the truthful torture that goes on.

In Florida and Idaho, a service letter is only required if the employee was discharged. Indiana, Maine, Montana, and Nebraska require service letters after a resignation.

With regard to reference letters, however, applicants

should know that almost all state laws restrict employees' access to references contained in their personnel files. These restrictions are intended to encourage candid assessments of prospective employees. But this confidentiality invites vindictive employers to retaliate against former employees by furnishing biased information. Some legislatures have attempted to solve this problem by requiring employers to give former employees letters of reference on request that truthfully state the causes for their discharge. Most of these laws also require the former employer to state nothing beyond the facts in the letter in later communications with reference checkers.

In some cases, laws punish employers for failing to provide the employee with a service letter on request, or falsely stating the reason for discharge or resignation. For instance, Florida and Montana require an employer to give the discharged employee a truthful statement of the reasons for his or her dismissal within 10 days after a written request. If the employer fails to do so, it is permanently prohibited from giving prospective employers any oral or written statement of the reason. If an employer does, it can be liable to the employee for an unlimited amount in a civil action and can also be criminally prosecuted.

Florida imposes a unique obligation on a prospective employer who receives a service letter or any oral communication. It must give the employee a copy of the letter or the substance of the oral communication within 10 days of a written request. If the prospective employer fails to do so, it too can be civilly sued or criminally prosecuted.

If you want to learn more about your legal rights after being terminated or when requesting reference letters, contact your state attorney general or labor department.

Generally, you are protected by law from intentional or negligent *false* statements about you or your reasons for leaving. But, in some states, employers don't have to reveal the contents of the references they receive about you. So, you may not even know that something false is being said.

If you present references using the guidelines we've discussed, you should be generating offers like an electromagnet. If not, there's a strong possibility that someone is short-circuiting them by saying something you don't like. If so, learn your rights under the antiblacklisting laws in your state, and shock your former employer with high voltage. Even if there are no statutory penalties for such action, juries throw the casebook at people like that. After all, who serves on jury duty? That's right—your working peers.

Here's how I answered an interesting inquiry for a reader of Joyce Lain Kennedy's nationally syndicated *Careers* column:

Dear Joyce:

What are my rights concerning the following:

I am a dental hygienist. The law in this and most other states says that I must be employed by a dentist. Full-time employment is difficult to find since full-time jobs require benefits. Therefore, most of us work for several employers simultaneously, but independent of each other.

Does Employer No. 1 have the legal right to contact Employer No. 2 without my permission to discuss me, my salary, my performance, and my personal life? Can Employer No. 1 try to discredit me with Employer No. 2 and to collude about pay, benefits, etc.? In general, can he try to get me fired so I remain in his office at the lower salary?

What can be done about this chronic problem? We are licensed professionals with almost no representation, because we are independent, yet dependent and physically isolated.

Thank you so much for your help and concern.

Sincerely,

Trudy

Dear Trudy:

Thank you for your inquiry to Joyce Lain Kennedy. At her request, here is my reply:

Employer No. 1 has a "conditional privilege" under the common law to discuss your job performance with Employer No. 2. This is *not* an absolute legal right, since the dialogue must be *reasonably related* to matters that concern your duties. Since the privilege is conditional, the scales of justice are balancing Employer No. 1's right to know about his employee against your right to privacy. The "reasonableness" depends on the circumstances—if he limits his discussion to factual, statistical data and objective professional opinions, he's probably "cloaked" with the privilege.

But when it comes to "discrediting" you with Employer No. 2, Employer No. 1 better be ve-r-r-r-y careful. Any false statement may render him liable to you for compensatory (to compensate), punitive (to punish), and exemplary (to set an example) damages. The latter two types of damages are *unlimited*. The primary theory used is *defamation* (of character). If the words are oral, it's *slander*, and if they're written it's libel. In fact, the courts recognize that injuring someone in their occupation is so dangerous that they often *presume* actual (compensatory) damages. The wrongdoing is known as "defamation per se."

What can be done? Your lawyer can file a lawsuit alleging such theories as **breach of contract, breach of fiduciary duty, inducing breach of contract (your employment), interference with contractual relations, interference with prospective economic advantage, conspiracy** (with Dentist No. 2), and a variety of statutory violations under state and federal labor laws. As you can see, Dentist No. 1 has drilled himself a very large cavity, and may find he doesn't have enough gold to fill it by paying you. He may get some help from Dentist No. 2, though.

Before you do anything, *confront Employer No. 1.* You may be pleasantly surprised. You won't need it, but GOOD LUCK!

Very truly yours,

Jeffrey G. Allen, J.D., C.P.C.
Director, National Placement Law Center

Chapter

14

How to Find Out Government Information About Yourself

You'd be amazed how much information on your personal, financial, and occupational activities is in the files and computer memories of local, state, and federal agencies. Much of it is there just for the asking, and employers ask constantly. Shouldn't you know what they know?

BLASTING INTO THE GOVERNMENT GOLD MINE

You may have to make some noise, but using this explosive is perfectly legal. It will blast you directly into the government gold mine of information about you.

Federal, state, and local government agencies guard the entrance to the mine. You might think that in a democratic society all you have to do is politely ask the guards to step aside so you can begin digging. Just identify the agency, then call or write to order the records. Right?

Wrong. You have to cut through the bureaucratic red tape and the possessiveness of some officials for government files. Also, people in all levels of government tend to bury information that may embarrass them.

The explosive to use for access to federal records on yourself is known as the Freedom of Information Act (5 USC 552), which became law in 1966. The FOIA represents an attempt by Congress to balance the right for anyone to obtain any available government-guarded information against the right (or necessity) of the subject of the information to prevent its disclosure. Most state and local governments have similar laws.

Using the FOIA requires the skill of a demolitions expert. You will need to use all of your powers of communication, persuasion, and compromise to break into the government's enormous information storage.

The FOIA started the Great Information Gold Rush on Washington. The most valuable ore has been Justice Department files regarding corporate mergers, acquisitions, and other maneuvers. (A bonanza if you are interested in doing some digging on prospective employers in your industry.)

FBI, CIA, SEC, and all other files are equally accessible. Court and Congressional files are not available through the FOIA, but most are published somewhere—you just have to find where.

While the FOIA doesn't define "records," the federal courts have done so consistently. They include every document, computer memory and readout, audio and video tape, photocopy, photograph, and so on—virtually every written and visual record ever made.

WHAT'S AVAILABLE

Following are four categories of information the government knows about you. Now you can learn about yourself before an employer does.

Criminal Records

These include arrests, pleas, convictions, fines, and sentences. The only time this information is not available is in the case of criminal investigation records when disclosure would impede the investigation, jeopardize the safety of officials, interfere with the rights of the subject, injure an informant, and so on.

Even in the case of dismissals, or records that are ostensibly expunged after a sentence is served, other agencies might still maintain those records. One jobseeker had been arrested the first time for a misdemeanor at the age of 18, pleaded guilty, paid a $60 fine, and served 100 hours of community service. The records were supposed to have been erased. He sent for his mug shots and fingerprints right away, and thought he was safe. He succeeded in college and his career, without so much as a traffic ticket.

Some years later, while working for a defense contractor, he learned that the FBI still had the information in its files. He discovered a private investigation service had been hired by his employer to monitor his "stability." If you've ever been arrested for anything, even if the charges were later dropped, check with the FBI to see if they think you're worth watching.

Civil Court Records

These include litigation initiated or defended, dismissals, judgments, satisfactions of judgment, and so forth. Actual pleadings in the official files are also often available. Prospective employers are often interested to know whether you've sued a previous employer, so it pays to check the accuracy of the records.

Driving Records

These include all known past addresses, social security numbers, violations, pleas, acquittals convictions, suspension, and revocations.

Another jobseeker had a critical error in his driving records, thanks to bureaucratic bungling. His state department of motor vehicles sent a notice of a court date for a minor traffic infraction to the wrong address. When he didn't respond, they sent a notice of suspension, this time to the right address. He cleared the matter up right away and his license was reinstated, but years later his driving records still reflected the suspicious suspension.

Educational Records

These records contain not only verification of degrees, but transcripts, attendance information, and the payment history on student loans. An attorney whose firm did a good amount of collection litigation worried that *her* delinquent student loan file would pass across her desk some day!

HOW TO FIND IT

You don't have to worry needlessly—you can find out what's there and correct any errors. This arsenal will help you conduct your own background check.

Automatic Publication

Some information you don't even have to request. It's already published somewhere, in one of thousands of government publications.

The *Federal Register* is your guide to the government's paper mill. You can find it in most public libraries. It contains indexes to everything in the text. The text explains everything regarding jurisdiction of an agency, how it operates, why, and other procedural information.

While this is great background information, it reads like a jobseeker's first attempt to write a resume. Since the *Federal Register* is a daily publication and contains millions of words you don't need, a better source for agency information is the constantly updated *Code of Federal Regulations*, also found in the library.

Semiautomatic Publication

This means "sometimes," but "always" if you know how to push the right detonator button. Agency findings, opinions, decisions, orders, and dispositions of cases are *available* (as opposed to *accessible*).

An invaluable prospector's map to the 7,500 government agencies that might have information you want is *The Guide to Background Investigations* (GBI), available for $95 from:

> National Employment Screening Service
> 8801 South Yale Avenue
> Tulsa, Oklahoma 74137
> (800) 247-8713

This will help you know what human resorcerers and executive recruiters know about you. However, unless you at least know the type of records you want or the geographical area where they are kept, you'll be wandering around aimlessly panning in the sand.

As I mentioned, the GBI lists 7,500 offices. That's 7,500 grains of sand—an endless shoreline with hardly a clue to finding the mother lode. But since this is about *you*, it should be easy to recall where you've been and what you've done. You can lead the gold rush and get there before some procrastinating prospective employer.

Ordering the Information

Once you find the exact spot where you want to drill, call the agency and ask:

1. The exact procedure for obtaining the file.

2. The cost to photocopy and send the file.

3. The full name, title, and phone extension of the person who gives you the cost and procedure.

The last item is by far the most important. Identify who is giving you the information—and don't assume anything about the competence of the person belonging to the voice on the other end of the line. (Don't assume *incompetence* either.) If you do, you may never see that document or your uncashed check. You're completely at the agency's mercy, so:

4. Write down the ordering information you requested.

5. Address your letter, referencing the check enclosed, to the person (including title) who gave you the ordering information.

6. Describe exactly what you want. A description is legally sufficient if a professional employee who is familiar with the area can locate the records "with a reasonable amount of effort." (You know what *that* means!)

7. State that your request is pursuant to the Freedom of Information Act. (This may avoid your being stone-walled by an "exemption.")

8. Ask the person whether a self-addressed, stamped envelope will expedite the request. If so, send it along and reference the enclosure in your letter. If not, *don't* send it—doing so may actually delay processing.

The FOIA requires that you receive some response within ten business days (with an extra ten if the agency informs you of "unusual circumstances").

TAKE YOUR CHANCES

The third and final way to investigate and retrieve government information about yourself is to take your chances that it's there and ask for it. This includes all records *not specifically exempt* from disclosure. They're supposed to be made "promptly available" to you.

Exemptions to FOIA

The exemptions in the following list will tell you if the agency official is bluffing or just not in the mood to go digging on the day you call:

1. National security matters (pursuant to an official Executive Order signed by the President).

2. Agency personnel policies (relating "solely to internal personnel rules and practices").

3. Trade secrets of businesses (if *voluntarily* given to the government and otherwise protectable).

4. Internal and external "agency memoranda" (poorly defined and subject to a major blast in a vulnerable spot).

5. Personnel data that would illegally invade a government employee's privacy under usual circumstances.

6. Criminal investigation records if, as noted earlier, disclosure would impede the investigation, jeopardize the safety of officials, interfere with the rights of the subject, or injure an informant. Once again, rulings on these items are arbitrary. (If you're the subject of the investigation, you can decide whether revealing the records to you would "interfere with your rights." In most cases, just the opposite is true.)

7. Financial institution data related to "examination, operating, or condition reports."

8. Statutory exemptions that state the reason *and* allow no discretion on the part of the agency.

Your Rights of Appeal

If you are denied access to records on the basis of any of these exemptions, you can inform the chief officer of the agency (by letter) within 30 days of your intent to appeal, or file an action (by lawyer) in the U.S. District Court having jurisdiction. Patience works in some cases. Pleading in others. Persistence in most. The agencies cooperate—eventually.

For more information on the FOIA, send for the free eight-page pamphlet entitled *The Freedom of Information Act: What It Is and How to Use It* from:

> Freedom of Information Clearinghouse
> P.O. Box 19367
> Washington, D.C. 20036
> (202) 785-3704

Correcting Errors

Once you have the records you requested, examine them carefully. If they are incomplete, inaccurate, or outdated, you have the right (which you should by all means exercise) to amend them. The agency must acknowledge your written request to amend the records within ten working days and must determine the merits of your request "promptly." If the agency issues a decision not to amend as requested, the same appeal rights are similar to those mentioned earlier. You must appeal in writing within 30 days.

YOUR RIGHT TO PRIVACY

In 1974, eight years after enacting the FOIA, the government created the federal Privacy Act (5 USC 552a). According to the PA, "Personal" records—such as those mentioned in this chapter—are those maintained by government agencies. The

PA was partially a response to the bonanza of personal records opened by the FOIA. In most cases, you will know if an employer or prospective employer is doing a background check because you will be asked to sign a release for it to do so.

A useful pamphlet is *Protecting Your Right to Privacy: Digest of Systems and Records*, available at no charge from:

Superintendent of Documents
U.S. Government Printing Office
Washington, D.C. 20402
(202) 783-3238

If you enclose $1.75 and ask for *A Citizen's Guide on Using the Freedom of Information Act and the Privacy Act to Request Government Records*, you'll be ready to start digging.

Your Right of Refusal

You have a right to refuse to sign a release pursuant to the Privacy Act. However, such refusal will set off employer investigation alarms. Instead, head them off at the pass by getting to the mother lode first, making sure the records are accurate, and then letting them go digging themselves.

One of the joys of jobseeking is that companies want to know about your past jaunts with public authorities. That's why Richard Long, in an article entitled "What's Missing from Most Background Checks" in the August 1988 issue of *Recruitment Today*, said: "Hard facts in the public domain— such as criminal convictions, histories of alcohol and drug abuse, or involvement in excessive litigation—can give substantial assistance in the employment screening process."[1]

In Chapter 15, we discuss how to seal the mines you can't blast—criminal record files.

Chapter

15

How to Go from Concealing to Sealing Your Criminal Record

It's perfectly logical to try concealing a criminal arrest or conviction. Nobody's perfect, but the irony is that applicants who conceal crimes are often the most honorable. Virtuous people tend to feel more guilty about an act such as lying, while others don't even consider it. People with something to hide are quite skillful at keeping their skeletons in the closet. They justify their actions by considering them omissions instead of lies.

Paul Ekman explained this rationale in *Telling Lies*:

> Not everyone considers concealment to be lying; some people reserve that word only for the bolder act of falsification. . . . When there is a choice about *how* to lie, liars usually prefer concealing to falsifying. There are many advantages. For one thing, concealing usually is easier than falsifying. Nothing has to be made up. . . .
>
> Concealment may also be preferred because it seems less reprehensible than falsifying. It is passive, not active.[1]

It's understandable that applicants try every possible avenue for concealing criminal arrests and convictions. Eating is such a compelling motive for concealment that no threatening words on an employer's application form about "falsifying or omitting information" stop a serious jobseeker.

Employers know this, so they check criminal records anyway. If there are fingerprints on your record, you probably interview poorly. Then you're mysteriously rejected or gently "ejected" without being told why. But you know. It's just that you never knew what to *do* about it. Well, now you will.

With your criminal records sealed forever, you'll interview better. The interviewer will sense your self-confidence, recognizing that it is real instead of acting. You will be able to vocalize your strengths and admit freely that you have weaknesses. You will see that your weaknesses will not affect your career.

Do you need to erase the past and resurrect your stage presence? If you're not sure, ask yourself the following ten questions:

1. Have you ever been convicted of a felony?

2. Have you failed to perform any obligation imposed on you by a court order resulting from conviction of a felony?

3. Have you ever had a professional license denied, suspended, or revoked?

4. Have you ever been reprimanded, censured, or disciplined by any professional licensing authority?

5. Have you ever been denied membership, suspended, or expelled from any professional organization?

6. Have you ever been reprimanded, censured, or disciplined by any professional association?

7. Have you ever been refused a bond in connection with your job?

8. Has anyone ever sought to recover against a bond for your conduct on the job?

9. Have you ever been suspended, expelled, or disciplined by any educational institution?

10. Have the records of any of these items been sealed or expunged?

Although the procedure for sealing criminal records is different for every jurisdiction—and you should check with the court where you had your encounter—following are the general guidelines.

IF CONVICTED FOR POSSESSION OF DRUGS

Drug possession crimes are *ten times more common* than any others. They're also treated differently from other crimes by federal and state authorities. That's why I treat them separately here.

Driving Under the Influence (DUI) or Driving While Intoxicated (DWI) cases are generally treated as traffic violations, although many states are getting tougher and making suspension mandatory even for a first offense. Still, cases heard under the older, less stringent laws should have little impact on your eligibility for employment.

If you were at least 21 years old and charged under federal law with possession of certain *controlled substances* (21 USC 812), your case may be *dismissed* and the records *sealed*.

To qualify, you must show:

1. No prior conviction of a drug-related crime.

2. No similar dismissal of a drug-related crime.

3. That you pled guilty or were found guilty of the possession of controlled substances.

Federal law [21 USC 844 (b) (1)] allows the judge to give a sentence that can prevent "guilty" from ever appearing on the court record. In such cases, the accused was placed on *probation* for a specified period (usually one year). If no *condition* of probation was violated, the court can *discharge* the person and *dismiss* the charges.

A sample Discharge and Dismissal Order is shown on the next page. Once the order is entered, the court records are

Sample Discharge and Dismissal Order

UNITED STATES DISTRICT COURT
FOR THE CENTRAL DISTRICT OF ILLINOIS

```
UNITED STATES OF AMERICA,     )
                 Plaintiff,   )
                              )   Docket No. CR 78-145-TLN
                              )
            - vs -            )
                              )
                              )
ARNOLD R. APPLICANT           )
_____ )
```

DISCHARGE AND DISMISSAL

THE COURT, pursuant to 21 USC 844 (b) (1)

hereby discharges Defendant from probation and

dismisses those proceedings under which probation had

been ordered.

Date _____   _____

                         JUDGE, UNITED STATES DISTRICT COURT

sealed (placed in a file or envelope, then permanently closed) and *archived* by the court clerk. The subject's name is removed from all *indexes* and *docket lists*. Only the U.S. Department of Justice keeps a (nonpublic) record of the dismissal, to prevent someone from seeking the same kind of dismissal more than once.

This procedure is extremely significant, since the applicant who goes through it can honestly answer "No" when an employer asks "Have you ever been convicted of a crime?" (Assuming, of course, there's no other conviction on his or her record.)

If a person is ever convicted of "possession" again, he or she will be sentenced as a *first offender*. After that, however, sealing the record under federal law is unlikely. Someone who seeks to do so will need the best lawyer he or she can find to *petition* the court. Fortunately, this is an area in which "public interest" legal clinics excel, so there may be almost no cost involved.

Someone *charged* with possession before the age of 21 has an additional remedy [21 USC 844 (b) (2)]. It's called *expungement* (literally "destruction"). After ten years, the sealed file is physically destroyed—forever. Even the Department of Justice doesn't retain the records. A sample Discharge, Dismissal, and Expungement Order is shown on the next page.

In *The Criminal Records Book* attorney Warren Siegel cautioned:

> Getting your criminal record destroyed is the most complete form of "record cleaning" available . . . [But] regardless of what's supposed to happen, sometimes agencies don't take papers out of their filing cabinets or entries out of their computers when they're supposed to. After several months have passed, we recommend you obtain copies of your criminal records . . . to see whether

Sample Discharge, Dismissal, and Expungement Order

UNITED STATES DISTRICT COURT
FOR THE CENTRAL DISTRICT OF ILLINOIS

UNITED STATES OF AMERICA,   )
            Plaintiff,   )
)   Docket No. 78-145-TLN
)
        - vs -   )
)
)
ARNOLD R. APPLICANT   )
_____)

DISCHARGE, DISMISSAL AND EXPUNGEMENT

THE COURT, pursuant to 21 USC 844 (b) hereby

discharges Defendant from probation and dismisses those

proceedings under which probation had been ordered.

THE COURT, having found that the Defendant in

the above-named action is qualified under 21 USC 844

(b) (2) for expungement of record, it is hereby ordered

that all recordation relating to the defendant's

arrest, indictment or information, trial, finding of

guilty, dismissal and discharge be expunged from all

official records to the extent required by 21 USC

844 (b) (2).

Date _____   _____
                     JUDGE, UNITED STATES DISTRICT COURT

the agencies have complied. If they have not, point this out to them and hopefully you'll get some action. All agencies have procedures to respond to requests for correction of mistakes in their records.[2]

States vary widely in their laws and procedures for prosecuting drug-related crimes. However, most have downgraded the possession or use of small quantities (usually less than one ounce) of marijuana from a felony to a misdemeanor. The typical punishment is a fine and informal (unsupervised) probation, followed by automatic destruction of the record usually after two years.

Some statutes even provide that, after satisfactory probation:

- A jobseeker can answer "No" to questions about a prior criminal record.
- A professional license cannot be denied based upon a conviction for limited marijuana possession.

IF CONVICTED OF ANY OTHER CRIME

When federal law is involved, the remedies for sealing records vary depending on:

- Severity of the crime.
- Type of conviction.
- Sentence imposed.
- Satisfactory fulfillment of probation.
- And other variables.

Because there are exceptions and limitations throughout the statutes, the advice of a criminal attorney should be sought.

State law is probably involved, as well. All states provide a procedure for *petitioning* a court for sealing records. Whether the petition will be *granted* depends on the answers to four questions. Here they are, along with the answers that usually apply:

1. Were you an adult when the crime was committed?

As with drug possession convictions, minors receive preferential treatment. This doesn't mean that sealing happens automatically, though.

If you were convicted of a crime before you turned 21, your first step is to request the record ("rap sheet") from the appropriate department, such as the county clerk. If it indicates that the conviction remains "of record," you should then contact the probation department. Someone there will often prepare the necessary papers, petition the court, and represent you, if necessary—at taxpayer expense.

2. Was the conviction for a felony, misdemeanor, or infraction?

I'm not talking about the crime *charged* here. A *plea bargain* (typically reduction of the felony charge in exchange for a guilty plea to a "lesser included" misdemeanor) is the same as the misdemeanor charge and conviction.

Many state labor or equal employment laws prohibit employers from asking about convictions for misdemeanors. So much for the law. Employers with interstate operations use forms that ask about misdemeanor convictions. Others use outdated forms. Still others flagrantly violate the law. Ditto for arrest information.

Even the most law-abiding, enlightened employers

have ways of picking up information about arrests, charges, and sentences for everything from smoking in the boy's room to bouncing a check at the market. Being enlightened, they just find another reason not to hire (or to fire if they already did).

3. Were you placed on probation?

In our overworked criminal justice system, many people don't even *realize* they were placed on probation! The judge bangs his or her gavel down, then, with the speed and diction of an auctioneer, says something about "unsupervised" or "summary" probation or "own recognizance" (or maybe just OR). The convicts pay the fine and rush out to find a parking ticket waiting on the windshield.

This becomes very significant, because in our system almost nothing happens automatically, including expungement of those records. That probation, long forgotten, can become an invisible ball and chain if you don't unearth the records and petition for their sealing or destruction.

4. Were you placed on parole?

There's a *big* difference between parole and probation, as anyone who has ever been on parole knows. Parole occurs *after* someone has been convicted and imprisoned, usually for a felony. There's always a *parole officer* and the records are easy to find.

The important questions here are:

- When did parole begin?
- Were there any parole violations?
- Were all terms and conditions of parole met?
- Are you still required to report to your parole officer?

If the parole has not ended, you're probably going to have to wait until it does, then proceed directly to the parole board for help in sealing the record.

IF A PROFESSIONAL LICENSE HAS BEEN DENIED, SUSPENDED, OR REVOKED

Applications for almost all state licenses carefully investigate anything that could even remotely reflect on someone's character.

Unlike pre-employment inquiries, the granting of a professional license is for the protection of the public. Therefore, protection from disclosure is virtually nonexistent. Let's look at all three situations.

Denial of a License

While this doesn't usually haunt you like a public record, it is easily checked. Approximately 30 percent of all applicants who say they have a professional designation in industrial occupations (engineering, physics, architecture, etc.) don't.

Professional licenses can be verified with one phone call. If an employer does make the call, there's an intentional misrepresentation, also known as *fraud*. That is "just cause" to terminate any professional employee anywhere.

Suspension of a License

Unlike denial, suspension is a matter of public record, because it usually involves a temporary removal of the license until there's a *hearing, restitution,* or *compliance* with certain conditions.

If *reinstatement* occurs, statutes vary widely in terms of

the extent and period of disclosure. Most are limited to ten years if there are no further incidents.

Revocation of a License

This rarely occurs without a *hearing, right of appeal*, and *entry of a final order*. Revocation is not only easy to check by phone, but public notice is usually given in official publications when revocation occurs.

Records of license revocations are particularly difficult to seal or otherwise remove, because:

- The budgets of licensing agencies are often tied to statistics. The more revocations, the bigger the budget.

- Protection of the public outweighs the right to privacy of the individual involved.

- Those with active licenses want to prevent those without them from practicing.

All of these tenets of licensure apply to *certification* by public or private entities, as well.

IF A PROFESSIONAL MEMBERSHIP HAS BEEN DENIED, SUSPENDED, OR REVOKED

The courts have generally held that membership in a professional (trade) association is not an enforceable right *unless* it is a prerequisite to actually working in the field. Then it becomes virtually the same as a license.

The U.S. Supreme Court ruled in *Gibson* v. *Berryhill* (411 US 546, 93 S.CT. 1689, 36 L.Ed.2d 488) that the Alabama Board of Optometry could not discipline a licensee because its members had a financial interest in preventing him from practicing. It was deemed to be a *restraint of trade* and violative of *due process*.

Most trade associations don't hold the keys to the office anyway. Suspension or revocation usually occurs after adjudication of some breach of contract or conspiracy allegation.

The cases vary so widely that no all-purpose laws apply. But one practical rule to be aware of is: Volunteers don't like to get involved in litigation. Therefore, there's much that a lawyer can do to set the record straight (or eliminate it).

As you can tell from reading this chapter, it's much easier to get into trouble than it is to get out of it once and for all. But it's not impossible, and you owe it to your references to try. And what better investment can you make than one you make in your future?

Endnotes

Introduction

1. *How to Turn an Interview into a Job* by Jeffrey G. Allen, J.D., C.P.C.

Chapter 1

1. *Interviewing for the Decision Maker* by Lawrence O'Leary.

Chapter 2

1. *How to Turn an Interview into a Job* by Jeffrey G. Allen, J.D., C.P.C.
2. *Ibid.*
3. *Conduct Expected, The Unwritten Rules for a Successful Business Career* by William Laureau.
4. *Op. cit.*

Chapter 3

1. *How to Turn an Interview into a Job* by Jeffrey G. Allen, J.D., C.P.C.
2. *Ibid.*

Chapter 5

1. *The Complete Q&A Job Interview Book* by Jeffrey G. Allen, J.D., C.P.C.

Chapter 6

1. *The Perfect Cover Letter* by Richard H. Beatty.

Chapter 7

1. *The Perfect Cover Letter* by Richard H. Beatty.

Chapter 8

1. *How to Turn an Interview into a Job* by Jeffrey G. Allen, J.D., C.P.C.

2. *Surviving Corporate Downsizing* by Jeffrey G. Allen, J.D., C.P.C.

Chapter 11

1. *How to Turn an Interview into a Job* by Jeffrey G. Allen, J.D., C.P.C.

Chapter 12

1. *Power! How to Get It, How to Use It* by Michael Korda.

2. *Winning Through Intimidation* by Robert J. Ringer.

Chapter 13

1. "See You in Court," by Donald C. Bacon, *Nation's Business*, July 1989.

2. *The Smart Interviewer: Tools and Techniques for Hiring the Best* by Bradford D. Smart, Ph.D.

3. *Ibid.*

4. *The Employee Termination Handbook* by Jeffrey G. Allen, J.D., C.P.C.

5. *Ibid.*

Chapter 14

1. "What's Missing from Most Background Checks" by Richard Long, *Recruitment Today*, August 1988.

Chapter 15

1. *Telling Lies* by Paul Ekman.
2. *The Criminal Records Book* by Warren Siegel.

Bibliography

Allen, Jeffrey G., J.D., C.P.C., *The Complete Q&A Job Interview Book*. New York: John Wiley & Sons, 1988.

Allen, Jeffrey G., J.D., C.P.C., *Surviving Corporate Downsizing*. New York: John Wiley & Sons, 1988.

Allen, Jeffrey G., J.D., C.P.C., *The Employee Termination Handbook*. New York: John Wiley & Sons, 1986.

Allen, Jeffrey G., J.D., C.P.C., *How to Turn an Interview into a Job*. New York: Simon & Schuster, 1983.

Allen, Jeffrey G., J.D., C.P.C., and Jess Gorkin, *Finding the Right Job at Midlife*. New York: Simon & Schuster, 1985.

Bacon, Donald C., "See You in Court," *Nation's Business*, July 1989.

Beatty, Richard H., *The Perfect Cover Letter*. New York: John Wiley & Sons, 1989.

Ekman, Paul, *Telling Lies*. New York: Berkley Publishing, 1986.

Hawkinson, Paul A. *Closing on Objections*. Research Information Bureau, P.O. Box 9653, Kirkwood, MO 63122. ($20.00)

Korda, Michael, *Power! How to Get It, How to Use It*. New York: Ballantine Books, 1975.

Laureau, William, *Conduct Expected, The Unwritten Rules for a Successful Business Career*. Piscataway, NJ: New Century Publishers, Inc., 1985.

Long, Richard, "What's Missing From Most Background Checks," *Recruitment Today*, August 1988.

O'Leary, Lawrence, *Interviewing for the Decision Maker.* Chicago: Nelson Hall, Inc., 1976.

Ringer, Robert J., *Winning Through Intimidation.* New York: Fawcett Crest Books, 1973.

Siegel, Warren, *The Criminal Records Book.* Berkeley, CA: Nolo Press, 1986.

Smart, Bradford D., Ph.D., *The Smart Interviewer: Tools and Techniques for Hiring the Best.* New York: John Wiley & Sons, 1989.

Index